JUL 1 1 2008

SANTA ANA PUBLIC LIBRARY

D0121786

GIANT

GIANT

THE ROAD TO THE SUPER BOWL

Plaxico Burress

with Jason Cole

B BURRESS, P. BUR
Burress, Plaxico.
Giant
        31994013843344

ENTERTAINMENT
An Imprint of HarperCollinsPublishers

GIANT: THE ROAD TO THE SUPER BOWL. Copyright © 2008 by Plaxico Burress with Jason Cole. All rights reserved. Printed in the United States of America. No part of this book may be used or reproduced in any manner whatsoever without written permission except in the case of brief quotations embodied in critical articles and reviews. For information address HarperCollins Publishers, 10 East 53rd Street, New York, NY 10022.

HarperCollins books may be purchased for educational, business, or sales promotional use. For information please write: Special Markets Department, HarperCollins Publishers, 10 East 53rd Street, New York, NY 10022.

FIRST EDITION

Designed by Renato Stanisic

Library of Congress Cataloging-in-Publication Data

Burress, Plaxico.
    Giant : the road to the Super Bowl / Plaxico Burress with Jason Cole.
      p. cm.
    ISBN 978-0-06-169574-2
    1. Burress, Plaxico.   2. Football players—United States—Biography.
3. New York Giants (Football team)   4. Super Bowl.   I. Cole, Jason.
II. Title.
    GV939.B83A3   2008
    796.332092—dc22
    [B]   2008016575

08 09 10 11 12 WBC/RRD 10 9 8 7 6 5 4 3 2 1

I dedicate this book to my loving mother, who passed on way too early in life. My mother was my earth, friend, teacher, dad, sister, and role model. To my family, my wife, Tiffany, and my son, Elijah, whom I love unconditionally—you are my strength, heart, emotion, soul, and life. To my brothers, Rick and Carlos—keep pressing! Keep your chin up, look people in their face, and don't be afraid to show people who you are. I love y'all. ALWAYZ!

—PLAXICO BURRESS

To Henry and Campbell, the greatest joy in my life.

—JASON COLE

CONTENTS

AUTHOR'S NOTE

First and foremost, I want the readers of this book to understand that these pages contain what society has presented to me in my life up to this point, leading to winning the Super Bowl. This is my personal story of what I've seen, felt, learned, learned from, how I have failed and achieved. Everybody has a story. This is the ONLY way I know how to tell it.

—PLAXICO BURRESS

Only One Way to Turn

It's three or four in the morning on Wednesday, January 30, 2008, four days before the Super Bowl, the biggest game of my life, and I'm asking, "What does this mean?" My left knee is swollen. It looks like there's a golf ball attached to the inner side of my left knee. New York Giants trainer and coordinator of rehabilitation Byron Hansen has just told me I have a grade-one sprain of the medial collateral ligament in my knee. All I know is that it hurts like hell and I can barely put any weight on my knee.

I've never had this, so I'm asking, What does this thing mean? They tell me the swelling will be there for like seven to ten days. I say, "Will I be able to play?" "I can't answer that question," Giants head trainer Ronnie Barnes says. I just bust out crying. How can this happen to me? It's going on Wednesday of Super Bowl week. I'm talking trash in the press all week. Now maybe I can't go on the field with my teammates and play with them? Can you imagine how that's going to look to the media—I predict we're going to beat the 18–0 New England Patriots and then I don't play?

This is how it is for me all season. From the start of training camp, when my left ankle was still recovering from surgery in the off-season, to the season, when I tore the ligament off the bone of my right ankle and shredded a ligament in my left pinkie, to when I separated my shoulder in the playoffs at Green Bay. My whole season is about playing in pain.

Then again, that's sort of what my whole life is like. When you grow up in the hood, you become immune to the pain. It's like sleeping through gunshots in the neighborhood. You just do it. We all deal with pain in this league. You better learn to play with pain. Still, there are a couple of times when I really think I'm going to have to shut it down, that I just can't play anymore this season.

I spend the next four days and even part of the Super Bowl wondering if this was going to be the time I have to stop playing. Wednesday morning is when I'm the most worried. Everybody who knows is worried. Hansen doesn't know what to tell me, Coach Tom Coughlin is freaking, and general manager Jerry Reese is worried. We all know one thing, though. We have to keep the New England Patriots from finding out.

This is how it works in the NFL. You have to keep the injury information hidden as much as possible. Especially now, with the championship on the line. I can't even tell people how I got hurt, stepping out of the shower on Tuesday morning, getting ready for media day. We're staying at the Sheraton Wild Horse Pass Resort and Spa in Scottsdale. Really sweet place. The showers are all glass on one side. As I'm stepping out of the shower, there are a couple of steps up and then you step out. As I push the door open and step out, my foot slides and gets caught under the door and I start to fall backward.

I'm trying to catch myself, but there's nothing to grab, so I fall and my foot gets caught under the door as I fall back. There is a little jolt of pain, but it doesn't feel too bad. We get to the stadium and we're waiting around, sitting and joking among the guys, and my left knee starts to get sore. I tell one of the trainers that I need a bag of ice. I ice it down and then we head out to do the interviews on the field at the stadium (the University of Phoenix Stadium, where the Super Bowl is to be played). There's thousands of people and they're all asking me about my prediction from the day before. Man, I didn't even know I was giving a prediction. But we're at the hotel the day before checking in and I walk through the hotel and some guy says, "What do you think about Sunday?" I say, we'll win, 23–17, and I didn't think anything about it. The next day, I get like forty text messages with everybody saying, "We're behind you, man, we love the prediction." I think to myself, *What prediction?* But I said it and now all of a sudden it's national news, so that's cool. I just go with it.

But when it's all done and we go over to take the team picture, my knee is still sore. So I'm leaving the field and I say, "Damn, something doesn't feel right."

I need to get another bag of ice and I tell Ronnie Barnes. I lean over and check my knee. But he checks it, too, and says everything seems okay.

As the day goes on, the pain gets worse and I ask Barnes to look at my knee again. No problem. So I go out that night with my teammates, returning to the hotel in time for the 1 A.M. curfew. I fall asleep but a few hours later wake up and the knee is worse than before.

About three or four o'clock in the morning, it's like *damn*, what is going on? I turn the light on and my knee is swollen. I get out of bed and my left leg is hurting so bad I can barely stand up. I pick up the phone and call Byron and tell him, "You need to come look at my knee." He comes down and pushes my knee around some more and that's when he figures it out.

Later on, I find out sometimes when you sprain the medial collateral ligament just a little, it doesn't even show up on an X-ray or MRI. They gave me another MRI and it showed up at that point. The good news is I don't need surgery. The MCL heals on its own. Even so, most guys miss one or two games with this injury, so I'm freaking. I worry about how I'm going to do this. I think, *I gotta play.* If I don't play and we lose, I'm going to look like a punk after talking all that shit. I mean, it's my knee and my career, but how can I not go out there?

The whole game plan is on me, even if I don't catch any passes. I'm supposed to go out there and take the double teams, draw two defenders in pass coverage, especially with tight end Jeremy Shockey out. Shockey was second to me on the team in receptions with fifty-seven when he broke his leg in the fourteenth game of the season. The coaches are distraught about it. But the first thing is making sure the Patriots don't find out about me. We practice later that day and the media is going to be there.

I take some anti-inflammatory pills and painkillers, but that's not doing much. I go out to practice and just jog a little, just straight ahead, no cuts, nothing. I catch a few balls warming up. But once the media is gone, I go inside and run in a pool to get a workout. The Giants list me on the practice report as missing practice because of my ankle and everybody buys it. Nobody knows, not even my teammates at that point, that my knee is messed up.

Me missing practice wasn't a big deal. I hadn't practiced all year. Not since the second game of the season at Green Bay, that is. Even in training camp I practice once a day every other day because I'm rehabbing my left ankle from surgery in the off-season. I don't play in any of the preseason games. But then I come out in the opening game against Dallas and score three touchdowns. We lose 45–35, but we come away feeling pretty good about our offense. The defense is still getting to know one another and learning the system, so they have a rough time. If we stop them or slow them down just once, we win that game. But then we go to Green Bay in the second game (on September 16).

My right ankle is already sore from training camp, but just before halftime, Packers cornerback Al Harris accidentally steps on my foot and the deltoid ligament in my right ankle rips right off the bone. On the very first play of that same game, I go to block Harris on a running play. He grabs my hand so hard it shreds the ligament in my left pinkie. The thing is now stuck. I can't extend it at all. Looks like a fishhook. Anyway, I play the rest of the first half, come back in the second half, but all I can do is about two plays before I have to sit down. From then on, I don't practice again during the week until December 26. So it isn't a big deal for me to miss practice.

Things get worse in the NFC Championship Game at Green Bay, that brutally cold game that we managed to survive. My teammate Amani Toomer said after that game that if you had any quit in you, that game would make you quit. The weather was brutal enough, but in the first half, Packers safety Atari Bigby hits me so hard that he separates my left shoulder. It's somewhere between a first- and second-degree sprain. Third degree is worse. There is one play in the first half after I hurt it where I had to hit the ground to catch a ball. As soon as I land, the pain shoots through me and I can't hold the ball. It's so bad I have to go into the locker room with twenty seconds left in the first half and get it shot up with a painkiller.

Just the shoulder injury alone probably should keep me out six to eight weeks, but I shoot that one up before the Super Bowl, too. It was completely numb, couldn't feel a thing. If I didn't do that, it would be painful the whole game. I would not be able to fight off a jam by the cornerback and it would be brutal if I landed on it. But that isn't the big deal. Getting through the knee injury is a much bigger deal.

Nobody notices that I have a problem with my knee. Everybody buys it when the Giants announce, "You know, his ankle is a little sore, so he couldn't go." My teammates don't know. Only Coughlin, the trainer, and GM Jerry Reese know. Not even the owners know at that point in the week.

On Thursday, I don't practice again. I do a little more, again not catching any passes in live drills, and then skip most of the rest of practice to work out in the pool. After practice, Coughlin tells the media I have a knee problem, but he says it is a lingering problem from during the season. He says, "Burress has an ankle that always is a problem, but he also has some issues with a knee that off and on in the past has bothered him. That's the thing right now. Between the two of them, that's why he's not working. He comes out and tries to go and can't go."

The funny part is that Coughlin is trying to play mind games with me at practice that day. He comes over to me before the practice on Thursday and says, "You're healed! You're healed!" He's kind of shouting it. He keeps talking, saying, "You're going to have one of the greatest Super Bowls in history, just great. You're going to have a big game." I just look at him like, "Dude, you're trippin." But they don't put me on the injury report at all that day.

Before practice, I tell the reporters I'm having a hard time, but still I'm not telling them how hurt I am. I say during the interviews, "It's pretty tough. I go through ups and downs. They ask me how I feel every day. I test it out. If it is a little sore, there is no need to beat it up and make it more sore going into the week. We take all the precautionary measures. I want to be as close to a hundred percent as I possibly can. We all know I won't be a hundred percent. I haven't been all year." But that's all I'm saying because it's a problem. I can't have the Patriots knowing there's something seriously wrong.

The other thing is that on Thursday they give me two or three braces to try. I've never worn a brace in my life and I can't wear them. I try them on and try to run, but they're too restrictive, too bulky. Plus, you can see it from a mile away. The Pats will know my knee is messed up if I wear that.

On Friday, the Giants put me on the injury report as "questionable" for the game with "knee/ankle" injuries. The only thing they say to the public is that I have fluid on my knee. There is nothing about an MCL sprain or tear, nothing about how I might be limited. The other thing is that by Friday, there are no more interviews with the players. We're off-limits to the press now, so I'm not taking any more questions.

I know all of this sounds supersecretive, but that's what it's all about. There is no sport like the NFL when it comes to secrecy. That's what the big story all year is. The opening week, the league busts New England for spying on the Jets and all hell breaks loose. It is in the news every week. Spygate this and Spygate that. Even that Friday morning when Commissioner Roger Goodell speaks to the media, it's like every other question was about Spygate, that whole scandal. Then we hear about how New England might have been spying on the St. Louis Rams back in 2001 before the Super Bowl, which sounds weird. That sounds like some serious balls.

But that's the whole thing in the NFL. You want every little tidbit of information you can get. Frankly, if the Patriots know how hurt I am, it might change the whole game. The thing about it is, if they know I have an MCL sprain, they know I'm not going to be able to plant on that leg. The MCL is the ligament on the inside part of the knee. It keeps the knee stable when you plant to cut and change direction. With wide receivers, we cut on just about every play. You can't just run straight lines all game. With those big offensive linemen, they can get by with it a little bit. They put those big braces on and they don't have to do much cutting or changing of direction.

My whole game is about being able to plant and cut. I'm six foot five, 227 pounds, so I can get an angle on just about any defender who tries to take me one-on-one. I'm not the fastest receiver in the league, but I'm fast for my size and the big difference is that I'm just as fast in and out of my cuts as when I'm running normal. When I cut, I can get two steps on a cornerback just like that. But what I can't do is cut on that leg and that is huge on my one big play of the game, the game-winning touchdown. I'll explain that later.

Anyway, on Friday, the Giants team doctor, Russ Warren, comes in and I see him. Warren is one of the most respected doctors in the league. He's been with the Giants since 1984 and he just lays it out for you. He doesn't BS around with guys, so guys trust him. Plus, he's been there longer than the coaches and the GM, so guys know he's not going to give in to them. Plus, there's like eleven other doctors with other NFL teams that worked under him, so you know he knows his stuff. He's like the Godfather of the NFL doctors.

What Dr. Warren says is the same thing Ronnie Barnes tells me. He tells me again that I should wear the brace, but I tell him I can't do that. I tell him, "Look, man, there is no way I'm going to be able to play with this pain. The painkillers and the anti-inflammatories aren't doing anything to really help me." I say, "What are my options for me to play in the game?"

Warren suggests I take an injection of Toradal directly to the injured part of the knee instead of continuing with the pills. The other thing is that the training staff comes up with another way to work my leg. Instead of putting a layer of padding over my leg before they tape it up, they say I should try applying the tape directly to the skin of my leg to make the wrap as tight as possible. The tape job runs from the bottom of my left thigh all the way to the top of my ankle. Still, Dr. Warren says that's not going to be enough support for the leg. So when he tells me about the injection, I'm like, "Let's do it." So they inject me. I wake up on Saturday and feel a lot better.

I went to the walk-through practice and I'm feeling better, but I guess I'm not really looking all that great. Jerry Reese, the Giants' general manager, doesn't say anything to me, but I hear what he says later: "It was really surprising to us that most of the early part of the week, it looked like Plax was not going to make it. Late in the week, he was still moving really gingerly, real slow. Usually by the end of the week during the season he was moving better, so I really wondered if he was going to make it, if he was going to play. I was really worried. I'm a spiritual man, so I pray all the time. The Lord is quicker than right now, so you're always praying to be in the good graces of God. As for mortal humans, I didn't think he was going to make it when I saw him on Saturday at the walk-through. He was moving very gingerly. On a scale of one to ten, on Saturday he was a three and that was up from a one the day before. Yes, I was worried."

After the walk-through practice, I'm still feeling better, but I talk to the doctor again. Dr. Warren tells me to take two tablets of Indocin. Indocin is a really powerful painkiller. I'm taking it all season to deal with the ankle injury, but I'm told to only take one at a time because it can really tear up your stomach—nausea, vomiting, all sorts of stuff. So I'm like, "Two? Are you serious?" But I take one on Saturday night before I go to sleep and the other on Sunday morning.

On Super Bowl Sunday, I don't feel any pain in my knee. I move it around and I'm like, "I might be able to go out there and give it a shot." I get to the stadium at roughly 1 P.M., about three hours before the game. The training staff does the tape job and I head out to the field for warm-ups. I start running, and it isn't long before I figure out how limited I'll be.

I can't cut to the right at all. Every time I plant my left foot in the ground and try to push my body to the right, the pain throbs so badly that I can't finish the move. I have to slow down every time. I go through part of the warm-ups and then head into the locker room to talk to the doctor again. I want to play, but I have to think about it.

The trainers take the tape off and tape it up again. I tell them I want it as tight as they could get it. And then the doc says, "If you are not feeling good about it, we can inject you again." I walk around for thirty minutes thinking about it. When I'm walking around, Coach Mike Sullivan, my receivers coach, says: "I care more about you than this football game. I know you want to play. But I don't want you to go out here and hurt yourself seriously later on down the road." Sometimes you hear people say that and they're just playing you, but not Sully. I know, deep down, he wanted me to play, but he really wants the best for me. We have a special relationship. When I first came to the Giants to visit before I signed, Sully was the one who came and picked me up. We hit it off right away at the airport. Sully is a military guy. He went to Army and he's gone to the airborne, ranger, and air-assault schools. Because of that, he looks at life the same way I do. You hear a lot of people refer to football as war and he's real sensitive to that because he has been to war. He understands football is not really like war, so he doesn't take it like that. He's all about life and family. He loves his daughter more than anything and I have never heard him raise his voice. He always just tries to talk to you. He knows football is not life and death. It's like I always say, football is the best temp job I'll ever have. Like me, he's going to get up, work hard, and do the best he can. He's not going to kill himself over a football game. Me and him, we're tight like that. I'll talk to his mom and she'll send me salsa from San Diego all the time. She makes it, freezes it, and sends it over. I talk to his wife and his daughter a lot. It's the best relationship I've ever had with any coach at any level.

So I'm thinking about what I'm going to do. I think about it and think about it and finally I say, "Let's do it," and shoot it up and numb it and it stays numb for maybe like the first half. Then I shot it up again at halftime. Here's a funny story about all of this: Two weeks after the game, I'm down in Florida. I have a place near Fort Lauderdale on the water. It's my sanctuary. I can't stay in New York after the season. I have to get away from football, all of it. It was the same when I was in Pittsburgh and I had a condo in North Miami Beach. Anyway, I'm down there training and I go see my physical therapist, Joe Caroccio. He runs Atlantic Rehabilitation Center, which is associated with the place where I train in the off-season, Perfect Competition.

It's two weeks later and Joe starts to go over all my injuries. He did all my work with me on my left ankle the year before, so he knows how bad that one was. He looks at my left knee. Then he looks at my right ankle, which has the torn deltoid ligament. In order for me to play, the trainers had to wrap the thing up really tight so that I was basically running on the side of my foot, then put all this padding under my foot to give me some kind of support. Eventually, I sprained the outside of that ankle, too. So I've got the torn ligament on the inside part of the ankle and then the sprain on the outside.

Both my legs are a mess and Joe says: "I don't know how you played in the Super Bowl. I don't know how you stepped on the field." He says in all his experience in this job—and he's been doing it since 1992—that he's never seen another athlete with these injuries who actually played. He just keeps saying, "I don't know how you did it."

During the Super Bowl, I'm scared of it. I don't want to tear my knee up. It's not worth it just to play in this one game. I'm scared as hell and then we go into halftime with New England leading 7–3 and it's like, "We are thirty minutes away from winning the world championship. If my knee is going to go, then my knee is going to go."

I wasn't much of a factor in the first half. My only catch was a fourteen-yarder. Of course that catch comes as I'm cutting to the left. They lined me up in the slot on the right and I run in across the middle and get the catch. I only had one other pass thrown to me and Randall Gay broke that up.

I cannot break to the right at all, but nobody figures that out. When I have a cover-two defensive formation and have to break to the right, I do it. But I'm in so much pain that I can't get open. None of the balls come to me. Now, break to the left—oh man, I can do that all day.

At the end of the third quarter, it's still 7–3. Finally, we put together an eighty-yard drive to open the fourth quarter and grab a 10–7 lead. Then the Patriots get an eighty-yard drive and they take the lead with 2:42 remaining.

That's when Eli Manning leads us on this amazing drive. We start at our seventeen-yard line. Right away we have to convert a fourth-and–one, but we do it. Then Eli comes up with that huge play on third-and-five. I'm running a sideline route just to clear out traffic. I look back and Eli disappears for a second and I think he's sacked, but then he pops out of there. By this time, I'm just jogging down the sideline and I keep going. Eli heaves the ball down the field toward David Tyree. I see David go up for it, but I don't see him come down with it pinned against his helmet. I don't see that until after the game. Just amazing. I think when he's going down there's no way he catches it, but he does. He leaps over Rodney Harrison, who's trying to punch it out, and he holds it.

That was the most physical-ass football game I have ever been involved in. I'm thinking that Rodney is going up there to cheap-shot David, knock some of the meat out of his taco. So when David makes that catch, I think, *We're going to win this thing*. We have the ball at the twenty-four. Eli hits Steve Smith on third-and-eleven and now we have it at the thirteen-yard line with thirty-nine seconds left. The whole thing is set up for my one big play. The call in the huddle was for a four-wide-receiver formation, three receivers (Tyree, Smith, and Amani Toomer) to the right and me by myself on the left.

I expect New England to have an extra defender on my side. They do that all game. But when I get to the line, all I see is cornerback Ellis Hobbs on me. They're in a defense known as "Cover Zero," as in zero help. More important, I'm running a fade pattern and I have all the room in the world to work with.

It's unbelievable. They're in Cover Zero and I've got like almost half the field to work this. It's just a great design. New England has Rodney Harrison blitzing, so I know I'm all alone with Hobbs. It's just a great call against what New England is doing. I look back and Eli is stomping his foot as fast as he can, trying to get the ball snapped before they change anything.

Hobbs is five foot nine, so I've got him by eight inches in height on this play. The fade is going to work. Worse for him, he's basically in a fifty-fifty situation. He has to guess which way I'm going and I see he's setting up for me to run a slant route to the middle. He still hasn't figured out I can't run that way. But I'm still going to sell him hard on it. Usually when receivers are setting up for a fade, they run these short, choppy steps, waiting for the cornerback to break. I come out really hard and fast, going right at him, like I was going to run a slant and break inside on him.

Hobbs dove inside. As he did, I broke outside. Hobbs couldn't recover. I didn't even see him after I made the move, but he just fell to the ground. Eli threw the ball up high and I was unchallenged. All I have to do is catch it. I think, *Oh my goodness, they must be baiting me*. I think I'm going to have to fight for it, but I make a move and I look up and the ball is just there, hanging in the air.

Eli threw the ball slightly behind me, which is pretty normal. When the ball is behind me, I usually do a quick turnaround, spinning my head around. But there's no way I'm taking my eye off this ball, so I turn the other way (clockwise) and watch it all the way in. I make sure I dragged my foot clear as day. As that ball is in the air, all I'm thinking is *Don't trip, don't trip*. I catch the ball and we're up 17–14 with thirty-five seconds left. I'm like, *How the hell did I get here?*

I remember after I caught that ball, I looked up at the ceiling of the stadium and I was thinking about my mom. I'm thinking about all the stuff we went through for me to get to this moment. I'm just thinking to myself, *I know who this is, that's my mom up there.*

2

One Tough Mother

I don't have a lot of pictures of me in my house in South Florida. I only have one picture of me playing football, from when I was twelve years old. When it all got started, I was playing in the community league back at Virginia Beach. Other than that, there's nothing of me playing football.

No pictures of much at all, really. Except one.

Downstairs is a big portrait of my mom, Adelaide. It sits on a stand in the entry room to the house. She's in her cap and gown from when she got her degree and became a nurse. You can see how proud and happy she looks. She was a great lady. Really proud and smart. She would make you think. I still cry sometimes when I talk about her. Every morning I come down and kiss that picture.

There are a bunch of wild stories about my mom. She worked hard to bring up me and my two brothers. I remember when I was growing up I used to say, "Damn, why is she so mean? Why is she so hard on us? Why is she so tough?" She was preparing us. Coach Coughlin is a walk in the park compared to my mom.

Mostly, she would just make me think. Still does. She died

on March 22, 2002. You know how when people say they can hear God's voice when they're praying? For me, it's my mom's voice I hear. I hear her telling me stuff, little sayings that make you stop and say, "What'd she mean by that?"

She was smart in terms of school, but she was also intelligent beyond book smarts. She would say something to you and you would be like, What is she trying to tell me? You wouldn't figure it out right away, but you'd think about it and then get it later. It would mess with you real bad. It's like when I was dealing with friends who were stealing from me early in my NFL career. I had this one friend of mine, he saw this $50,000 watch I had and he said, "Hey, can I borrow that to wear?" Now, this is a guy I've known since we were seven or eight years old. We know everything about each other, been through a lot together.

A month goes by and I call and leave him a message. He doesn't get back to me. Another message. No call. A year goes by before I hear from him and he doesn't say anything about the watch. I'm like, that's the way it's going to be? Damn, if he had just asked me I probably would have given him the watch, but he throws away all those years of being friends for a $50,000 watch. It was sad, man, and it ruins it for everybody you're around. You can't trust anybody. I had other friends from when I was growing up, they'd come stay with me when I got started in Pittsburgh. I'd come home and there's a check missing from the middle of the book. Stuff like that.

So I talked to my mom about it and the thing she said, and it's been with me ever since, was "Don't think with your heart, think with your mind." That's how I've tried to be ever since. You roll things around in your head before you say something or you think about what you're going to do before you just say yes to somebody who is your friend.

Her getting me to think started much earlier. It's like when she said to me, "You can't burn the candle at both ends." I didn't know what she was talking about. What the hell does that mean? But she said it to me when I was coming home early one morning in high school. It was after midnight and we had a regional play-off game the next day. I came in about one-thirty in the morning. She was up reading and studying and she said, "Boy, don't you have a football game today?" I said, "I'll be all right." She said right back to me, "You can't burn the candle at both ends."

Later, I figured out what she was telling me. What she was saying is that I couldn't be great at football *and* hang out on the street. You can't do both and she knew what she was talking about. You can't be great and party all the time. That is what it means to me now. You can't be a great football player, a great husband, or a great father and be out all the time. You have to get your rest. You've got to set your priorities. It just applies to so many things.

Sometimes I think about all the things she used to say to me. I struggle spiritually with it. I want to do something and she will be telling me don't do it and I do it anyway.

Then I sometimes think I'm second-guessing myself, but I'm not second-guessing myself. She is telling me what to do.

And my mom didn't take any shit. The people in the neighborhood didn't mess with her. It didn't matter if they were drug dealers, hoodlums, whoever. She didn't back down to no one. When they would see her on the street they would say, "Hey, how you doing, Miss B?" She knew everybody's name and they knew her name.

There's one of my favorite stories about her and it just says a lot about how she looked at life, how much pride she had. My little brother Carlos, he was born really prematurely. She used to say that she brought him home in a shoe box, he was so little. He still suffers a lot because not everything about him physically and mentally developed properly. He's probably at like a seventh-grade level. When he was real young, he was real skinny, so the other kids would call him "Ethie," like he was Ethiopian and starving. We'd come down out of the apartment or the house and they'd say, "What's up, Ethie?" One day my mom is with him and she hears that and she just snaps at them, "His name isn't motherfucking Ethie. Tell them your name, boy." Then he says in this really meek voice, "Carlos." Me and my one friend still laugh about that to this day. You just didn't mess with my mom about stuff like that.

For us boys, we were scared to get into trouble. That's why I was scared of calling her to tell her I got a girl pregnant. That was like my worst fear, to have to say, "I got a girl pregnant." She always said, "Don't bring no babies in here." My mom didn't take no crap at all. She would come to the high school basketball games and I will guarantee you to this day that everybody knew who she was from the opening tip. After the game she couldn't even talk. This was like every Friday night. And the referees, oh man, she would come out of the stands sometimes pointing to the referees.

There was this one time we were playing basketball in high school. I played for Green Run High. We were all black and our school would be in the news all the time. Guys would get busted for shotguns, bombs or fights, or whatever. There was something happening like once or twice a week. So instead of calling us Green Run, the other schools would call us Gang Run.

Anyway, we were pretty tough. We were playing this predominantly white school at their place and they held up signs saying GANG RUN. I had a breakaway layup and one of the guys from the other team comes in and undercuts me. It was pretty grisly and I sprained my wrist pretty bad. I'm yelling and cussing and get kicked out. This guy from the stands yells out, "You get what you deserve," and I get so mad now I'm going after him. They get me out, but on my way out of the game, I looked back and my mom is going into the stands to go get him. The police had to stop the game because my mom was going into the stands. It was incredible. That's how she was. Man, what a woman.

Her thing was always about how if you don't stand up, you fall victim. My mom was kind of like the community leader for the whole thing. With the girls in the neighborhood, she formed a step team to give them something to do besides having sex and getting pregnant. They actually became very good, won some first-place trophies.

She was kind of the force of the neighborhood. Everyone knew who my mother was, even my teachers. My teachers would say, "I saw your mother last night at the game."

I'd say, "What did she say?"

"Well, I can't really say exactly what she said," they'd answer. The teachers loved my mom. She was a show.

And you better not get in trouble. If you did something stupid, you didn't want to mess with her. She didn't whip our butts, she would challenge us to a fight. Just punch me right in the chest and say, "Come on, fight me." It would really hurt and there was no way you wanted to fight her.

When I was about fifteen or sixteen, we'd go to this one place toward the way back of the apartment complex, hanging out and playing spades. We'd turn the music up as loud as we could and there were girls there hanging out, a little drinking. My mom heard about what we were doing. So I'm sitting there one day with my back to the door when we hear a knock. Everybody is like, "Come on in." All of a sudden she came in there and she snatched me up out of my chair and pushed me and smacked me on the back of my head all the way home. She was saying, "I never want to see you there again. You don't hang out there playing spades. You don't know what you're doing." That's how she was and that was the last time I hung out there. Walking to school the next day, the guys all said to me, "Damn, you got your ass beat." Everybody knew what type of person my mom was.

At the same time, you didn't always know how she was going to handle stuff.

Where I grew up in Virginia Beach, Virginia, it was all drugs and crime. Like I said before, there were shootings and killings all the time. There was gunfire so random at night you just became immune to it. We lived in this place called Twin Canal at one point. It was public housing. My mom paid like a dollar a month for us to live there.

It was like one of the places where if you were a resident, you could come in. But if you weren't, you couldn't come in. They had police checkpoints you had to go through before you could come into the neighborhood. If your name wasn't on the list, you couldn't come in. Of course guys would sneak in all the time. There was this canal around the back side. The canal wasn't that deep, maybe three or four feet, and probably twenty-five yards across. I would see guys running across it, coming to sell drugs, buy, or whatever they could do. Maybe see their girlfriends.

The police would patrol the housing complex on horses. They would ride around in the canals and stuff. Some nights I would sneak out and I would go through the back to go have fun. This would be like one or two o'clock in the morning. Then I'd come back like at three or four in the morning and I had to make it back. My mom would never know I was gone. I knew I had no business being out there and then it would be like, man, I just got to make it back there. It was like a hundred, maybe a hundred and fifty yards and I would run as fast as I could, just hoping I didn't get hit by a stray bullet.

I hoped I didn't get caught in the craziness. I remember just standing outside hanging out, seeing a drug deal going down, and I guess the guy, it was a white guy in the car, I guess he had borrowed the money from one of the dealers and didn't have it to pay back or something. I just pore over this one so many times. I couldn't really tell what was going on, but the guy standing next to the car starts punching the guy who's driving. The guy in the car starts driving. He starts going like twenty, twenty-five miles per hour and the other guy is just hanging on. Finally, the guy hanging falls off and lands on the street. He stands up, pulls out his gun, and *boom, boom, boom*, he shoots out the back of the dude's window. I was like, *Damn*. I was only like twelve or thirteen seeing this. This is a rough place.

They didn't kill him, but there was this one time a good friend of mine, Diedrick, he got shot in the head. He was twelve or thirteen. It was random, he was just walking home.

I go by there just about every time I go home, just to check it out. Some of the guys I grew up with are still out there. They are standing on the corner doing the same thing. Their eyes are all yellow from the drugs. This is almost fifteen years ago now and they're still doing the same thing. There is a little 7-Eleven on the corner of the neighborhood. They're still stealing stuff out of there. I guarantee you I'll still see five or six guys I grew up with. I'll see one of them and they'll be like, "Hey, man, can you buy me some beer." I'll do it.

That could be me. I almost couldn't go to college, my grades were so bad.

It wasn't that I wasn't smart, but growing up in that place was really all that I knew. I wasn't thinking about going to school. Those people that we would watch on TV, they weren't real.

What was real was the guys smoking crack out of a Pepsi can under the stairwell, taking shits and pisses under there. It smelled horrible. I'd come out of our place every morning seeing that as I was going to school. I grew up seeing that and there was no way I was going down that road.

To be honest with you, thinking about all the people my age there, I was the only guy who played sports. For a guy like myself, there was really only one way out. Sports. Still, me going to college wasn't even an option at first. When I got my first recruiting letter when I was a sophomore, I looked at it and said, "This is a joke, I'm not going to college."

There were a lot of wonderful athletes who came from around where I grew up. Michael Vick, DeAngelo Hall, Allen Iverson. David Wright of the Mets is from Chesapeake. The Upton brothers. You go back in the day, you got Bruce Smith and Lawrence Taylor. Tons of guys. But when you come from neighborhoods like mine, a lot of guys just don't make it out.

We had this one little guy named Andre. We called him "Worm" in basketball because he was so good with the ball that he would just worm his way through your whole defense. He was younger than me. When I was a senior in high school he was a freshman. He got killed a couple of years ago. He had a nickel bag of marijuana and got shot six times in the chest. He was a little dude, wouldn't hurt nobody. His ball-handling skills were so elite.

There was this other time when I was going around the corner to see one of my friends, Wayne. It was about nine o'clock at night. I'm walking to his place and I can see two guys about to knock at his door. It's a loud knock and I can see that these two guys are standing at the bottom of the stairs. These are two guys I grew up with and they lived about twenty minutes away. I knew it was about something like how he owed them some money. I can just feel it. And I just know that as soon as he comes through that door, they're going to start shooting. They knock on the door. I can't say nothin', but I'm thinking, *Wayne, please don't come out of this door 'cause there's no way to get out.* The only way out is to go down the stairs to where those guys are at. My heart is beating like crazy, but he doesn't open it and eventually they walk away.

But I was a superstar, so the drug dealers would take care of me a little, give me a little money here and there. My friend Johnny, he would give me a little weed to sell, probably forty or fifty dollars' worth. He would say, "You don't have to give it back to me." Back then, forty or fifty dollars was huge, that was rich. When I saw how easy it was, it was too good to be true. The drug dealers, these guys had the cars with the fancy rims, they had the bad girls. They were hanging out on the weekend, going to the adult clubs when I was playing ball. You know that is what everyone catered to.

They were all cool about it. They all sold weed and crack. They all had pistols and guns, but I was the one, I was the oddball. I skipped school sometimes to hang with them, but I wasn't the one drinking and smoking. I just hung around with them because they were the guys in my neighborhood. I hung with them and they didn't look at me any differently. We were all cool with one another. But sometimes there would be a situation where someone would owe someone some money and it was about to get bad. These were guys older than me and they would say to me, "Hey, man, just go home, we'll come get you later." I would say I'll come back out in an hour. I would hate to have them come to my door because my mom would look at them with a bad look.

Then one day my mom was going through my pants and she found it. She found two empty bags and smelled it. I told her I didn't know what it was. She knew. She just went into her room and cried. That's when I thought about how hard she worked and I realized how guilty I felt. She handled everything differently. She cried and it hurt me so bad. She's working this hard for me and I'm doing this in return. I probably did it for about a summer, but once she found it, I quit. I still hung around everyone who did it. I knew what it was all about.

I was afraid of my mom. I was scared to death of my mom. I was like, I can't even imagine picking up the phone and telling my mom to come pick me up from jail.

She put that much fear in me as a son and as a person. I was afraid and then I didn't want to do wrong by her. She was the only person out there I was afraid of. Like I said, she would fight me.

She wouldn't whip me. She would punch me. She would snap me with a wet dishrag. She would pinch me. Then she would want me to hit her back. She would hit me hard and I thought about it, but I knew I would be in for a whipping if I did. She wasn't afraid and she wasn't backing down and that is why I didn't choose that path. I was like, man, I cannot pick up the phone and call my mom to get me out of jail just because I want some fast money. But that one time when she found the bags, she didn't fight me. Like I said, she handled things differently.

We moved around a lot. We didn't have a lot of money to be in a stable place all the time. My mom and my family, it was living paycheck to paycheck. Growing up like that, you don't understand why you're moving. You're just doing it. I thought that was how it was supposed to be. We were so young. We were in elementary school, so we didn't understand why we were doing it, we just knew we were. I'd go from one school to the next and have to make new friends all the time. That's how I know so many people from back home. I lived in damn near every bad neighborhood you could live in. I went to like six different elementary schools. One year, I went to four schools. I ended up finishing at the same place I started. It was just always a struggle, moving every three months or so sometimes. We'd move in with my grandmother Louise Elliott every once in a while.

My mom ran track at Norfolk State. I went by her high school last year and she still holds all the records for scoring in basketball and track. She was invited to be on the U.S. field-hockey team for the Olympics, but she couldn't go. I actually looked it all up. Mom was an animal, a beast as an athlete. She was about five foot ten, a beautiful lady, beautiful complexion. When she had me she was about twenty-five or twenty-six. She said it was her first time and she got pregnant.

I can only imagine how hard she worked. I was taking care of my son, Elijah, for three days one time when my wife, Tiffany, was out of town. After three days, I was ready to quit. I was exhausted. I wasn't physically tired, but, oh man, was I mentally beat. It's like pushing yourself and pushing yourself when you ain't got no more gas. You got to run one more sprint and you know you don't have it, but you just got to do it. It's mentally exhausting. I can't imagine what she went through taking care of three boys.

My mom drove a public school bus for thirteen years. What I remember most is we would get up at five-thirty every morning to ride the bus with her. She'd start with the high school run, then middle school, and then do the elementary school. In between, she'd drop us off because we didn't have a ride any other way. The school bus wouldn't come into our neighborhood. She'd get done around nine-thirty, go home and rest, and then do it all over again starting at one-thirty. After school, we'd go over to a friend or a relative's house and just play basketball every day until she came to get us.

She actually went back to college and got her master's degree in nursing when she was thirty-five years old. She went to school for three years so that she could get a better job. Those three years that she was going to school were the roughest. She was working at a gas station when she wasn't going to school. That was like the hardest time for us. But she chose to go back to school so that she could get a better job in the long run. Who has the motivation to do that at thirty-five? To go back to school and get her master's and then go through three years of odd jobs, like working in my uncle's antiques shop on the weekends, making maybe fifty dollars a day, a hundred for the weekend. Her goal was to just get us through all this.

I would come in her room late at night and she would be studying. She'd go through the books until one or two in the morning studying. She got all A's, aced biology. She didn't make one B. That's how intelligent she was. Still, it was a long struggle.

Sometimes we would come in the house and she would cook.

We would never even think about *her* eating, we would just eat up all the food. We would say, "Mom, you didn't eat," and she would say, "I already ate," not telling the truth. I never figured it out until she passed away. She went all the time with nothing because we didn't have enough food. She was strong. Her faith never wavered.

When my mom died, I wanted to quit football. I was so sick inside. I was twenty-five and I was burying my mom. The worst part is that if she had just told me how sick she was, I could have gotten her better care. She didn't tell me and I didn't see it. I still think about all that.

My rookie year in 2000, she came to all my home games and everything was fine. I got hurt that year, but she was there. In 2001, she started getting real tired doing normal things. In the back of my mind, I knew something was wrong, but she wouldn't let nobody know. She stopped going to the games. I said, "Mom, why did you drive all the way to Pittsburgh and not go to the game?" She said, "I'm tired, I'm going to stay here and make all the food, and everything will be all spread out for when you get back after the game."

For the whole year, she came to one game and then she was saying how tired she was. Walking up the steps was a strain. She was getting ill the whole time.

My uncle Andre knew, but my mom told him not to tell me what was going on. I was upset with him for a long time about that. They all thought they understood. She was sick, but I never knew until February 2002.

I had come home after the season in Pittsburgh. She seemed like her normal self.

She would get up, run her errands, go do things she wanted to do, and she would come home. Then I'd take off for a while. I stopped in Atlanta for a while, then left and flew to the Grammys in Los Angeles.

My brother Carlos called and said I needed to come home. He said, Mom ain't feeling good. So I called my mom and said, "What's going on, you ain't feeling good?" She said, "I'm fine, I'm a little tired, but I'm okay." I thought that was the end of it. Later that day, my other brother Ricardo called and said, "I don't know what Mom is telling you, but she ain't looking good, you need to come home and check it out."

I called my mom back the same day and said, "Hey, Mom, look, if you ain't feeling good, you need to tell me." She said, "I told them I'm fine, I'm just a little tired, blah, blah, blah." The next morning the phone woke me up out of a dead sleep. It was my uncle Adrian Elliott calling me and he was like, "Hey, man, look, you need to come home. Your mom is sick and you need to come home." When he said it that sternly, I was like, something is wrong, I need to go home.

I got up and I left. I didn't have my checkbook and my damn credit cards were like at a $2,000 limit at that time. I had to catch a first-class flight, but my debit card wouldn't work, so I had a starter check and they took that. Just let me on. I left Burbank at 7 A.M., but I had stops in Las Vegas and St. Louis, so by the time I got home it was 7 A.M. the next day.

When I got home I couldn't believe what I saw. My mom had lost twenty pounds. Her hair was falling out. What in the world was going on? I was sick, I was like, *Oh, no!* I had just been home three weeks ago. She was like, *Hey, baby,* like nothing was going on. That was her. She acted like everything was okay. Finally she told me, "I have a blood clot in my foot." My mom was a diabetic. She was pretty good about keeping up with it, but the way I was told, people sometimes get those clots no matter what. Her foot was wrapped up in gauze and it was practically dead because it wasn't getting any blood flow. When she said that to me I knew that back in 2001 that had been the problem. That's why she was getting tired going up and down the stairs.

That's what was going on the whole time, but she never told me. I couldn't believe she was in a wheelchair. I had to take her downstairs in a wheelchair. She had a doctor's appointment the next day, but she wouldn't let me take her. She got back home and I had to be there to bring her back into the house in a wheelchair. That's how bad she was doing.

The next day she told me she had to get her foot amputated. I said, *"What?"* She went to get her foot amputated, it all happened that quick. If I hadn't come home, my mom probably would have died before I ever saw her again. It happened that fast. She was sick for a while, though, but she chose not to tell me. I understand that, but my mom didn't really understand the help she could have received or the help I could have gotten for her.

She went in to get her foot amputated, and when they started the procedure, the doctors discovered her whole leg was infected, so they had to take it off right below the knee. I was there for the surgery and for a few days after. She was back talking like her old self, doing really well. She said, "Baby, I'm fine." So I rounded up my troops and packed my bags. We headed down to Jacksonville, Florida, where I'd been leasing a place for a while. I was down there because Fred Taylor is one of my best friends. We both got recruited by Florida and he ended up being friends with one of my best friends from back in Virginia, Cedric Warren. Cedric played at Florida with Fred, too.

We got all my stuff from Jacksonville and then headed down to Miami Beach, where I had just had a condo built. I got into the condo and I got down on one knee and gave thanks for what I've got. My mom always taught me to do that. It's me, my cousin T, Fred, and my best friend, Kevin Graves. We were all getting ready to go out and I jumped into the shower.

When I came out, everybody was crying. I said, "What is going on?" Nobody would tell me until I went to my cousin. I just knew as soon as I looked at him. My mom was gone and I was so sick. I felt so bad because I wasn't there. I think that is why it hurt so much. I wasn't there. I didn't know how I was going to play football anymore. I didn't care about anything.

I was twenty-five and burying my mom. I had to put everything together myself. It was hard. Tiffany—my wife now, but then we were just starting to go out—was the first person I called. She thought I was joking. She had just met my mom a few weeks before that. My mom really liked her. Tiffany busted out hollering and crying and I was crying so bad.

About a week after, we had the funeral. My aunt Mary did the eulogy. She's a minister. I spoke, too. I remember I stood up, there were probably two hundred people at the service. I didn't have a piece of paper with what I was going to say. I was speaking from the heart. I remember I said that when I was growing up, I'd be in my room crying so hard and asking, "Why is she so hard on me?" I realized at that moment, she was like that because she was preparing us for the day when she would pass on. She was prepping us to be adults, passing the torch. The other thing I talked about is how there were three things she said to me and that now I really understood them. She always said, "Don't take anything for granted," "You can't burn the candle at both ends," and "God will never put you through anything you can't handle." I said as long as I apply those three things in my life, I will do just fine. Then I walked offstage.

A lot of people didn't think I would get up and speak. But I had to. I cried so much the day we buried my mom. People came up to me the whole day and said, "Hey, man, the torch has been passed down." It was emotional to me. My brothers were in worse shape than me. Especially my brother Carlos, you could see he wasn't the same person. I had to get myself through this because they weren't going to make it without me. They were more screwed up than I was. They were with her every day I was in college and living in Pittsburgh. I would say to my brothers, "Hey, man, everything is going to be all right." They would cry for hours and I would listen. Then, when they left, I would cry, too. I never let them see me cry. I still cry.

When I think about it sometimes, and it makes me upset, I can only imagine how she would have been toward my son, Elijah. We wouldn't need no nanny, no cook, no nothing. I could hear her right now: "Why you all paying that money? I could do it." It would be like it was her child. I can only imagine how she would be toward him.

I go back to my neighborhood a lot. I usually go train there one week before we start camp. I hold Thanksgiving dinners there every year and I'm trying to build an after-school activities building in my neighborhood. I don't want to be a fairy tale. I want to be someone the kids there can see and touch. I think that's very important to them. I didn't have that when I was growing up. I'd watch athletes on television, but I didn't believe that kind of life was possible for someone like me.

I thought they were all fairy tales. I thought they were all make-believe when I was young. I saw them on TV, but I didn't think they were real people. I don't feel I owe anything to anyone outside of my neighborhood. I still go back to Michigan State and talk to the guys there, but as far as me trying to help the youth, it's about my neighborhood.

The way I grew up, we had hard times, we had rough times. But I have no regrets about how I grew up. I wouldn't change a thing. My mom, she would never have done anything to hurt anybody, but she didn't bow down to no one, either. She was my hero.

3

Finding Football

My coach at Green Run High was Elisha Harris. He's how I came about the idea for my son's name. He was so influential to me back then. I played guard in basketball when I was in high school and that's what I thought I was going to do. I just played football because everybody else, like my friend Cedric Warren, played. I *loved* basketball.

My high school coach, he put me on the football field. I just wasn't a real football dude. I played basketball every day growing up. I played football when I was younger, but I didn't take it serious. But I went out for football and it was fun at first. By my sophomore year, I started getting letters from South Carolina and Clemson. I was like, man, I'm barely a junior, I'm not even good.

Here's a good story—I got my first college letter when I was sitting in ISS. That's in-school suspension. I was suspended, but it wasn't serious enough that I had to stay home. It was the first day of my junior year. What happened was that on the last day of school the previous year, when I was a sophomore, me and some other guys got caught skipping school—on another school's property. There I was—the town superstar in football and basketball, I was like six foot five and I didn't think I was going to be recognized when I showed up at some other school. I don't know what I was thinking about, but I probably wanted to check out the girls at the other school, see what they got over there. I was crazy back then. As soon as we walked through the doors at the other school, the security guys grabbed me. So I didn't even know they gave me in-school suspension until I got back for the first day of junior year. I was in my new outfit for school and I was told I couldn't go to class.

So I got my letter and I wasn't really taking this seriously. I had an okay sophomore year, like eight or nine touchdowns, maybe seven hundred yards receiving. I was just so raw, all I was doing was playing. I played nothing but receiver, really, until my junior year.

I got to play free safety when I was a junior. I was a bad boy, man, real mean. But that junior year, I remember I was going through two-a-days and hating it. So I just walked off the field. I thought, Man, it's too hot, I don't want to play football. I'm a basketball player. So I got home and my high school coach came over to my house. He said, "Hey, you're the best player I've ever coached." I'm like, "What are you talking about? I just play just because my friends are playing." He said: "Son, you are a natural, God-gifted, born receiver. You are a natural." He just repeated that.

My mom was sitting there, and she's like, "Why don't you go play football?" I start talking about basketball and she said, "Well, you can do both." So I said okay. I went back out there the next day and played. My junior year was when I really took off. It was just like nobody could cover me; I was faster than everybody. I was All-State. I was all-everything. I was even defensive MVP of the team.

I had a good year and then my senior year all these magazines came out and I was on the front cover. I was the number one receiver in the nation and I was like, "Are you serious?" The other thing Coach Harris did, he pulled me to the side one summer day after I walked into practice and said, "Hey, I want you to sit down and look at this." He showed me a tape of Michael Westbrook and J. J. Stokes, who at the time were two of the best guys in college. I didn't know Westbrook at the time, but I knew about Stokes. Westbrook went to Colorado, was the number four overall pick in the draft in 1995 and Stokes was number ten that same year. Stokes went to UCLA. My coach says, "You are better than these guys. I want you to go to some [college summer] camps." I said, "Okay, I'll go to UCLA camp." It was a full-contact camp, but the State of Virginia didn't allow you to go to any full-contact camps. So we went up to Virginia to a camp and I just wowed them. Then I went to South Carolina and wowed them.

Then I went down to the University of Florida. I remember getting down there and running back Bo Carroll and quarterback Jesse Palmer were there. We were all still in high school and all these guys were talking about was Florida, Georgia, and Texas football. So I said, "Oh, y'all couldn't start at Virginia." They looked at me like I was crazy. Florida, Texas, and Georgia football were supposed to be real big. I was playing in Virginia, but nobody knew about that. Man, when I tell you I went there and ripped that camp to pieces, I ripped it to pieces. Then the Florida defensive coordinator at the time, Ron Zook, and another Florida coach, they beat down my door for seven months after that trying to get me to come to Florida. I wanted to go bad, but it just didn't happen. It didn't happen because UF didn't recruit guys who didn't meet academic standards. But I ripped the camp up. I got Most Athletic Camper, the Most Outstanding Player of the camp. I was playing quarterback, receiver, running back, free safety. I was just playing it all. Yep, quarterback. It was basically flag football, and back then I was so fast and so tall, I just dominated.

So I got back home and I was the number one receiver in the nation. Now everybody is trying to get me to come to school and play. That's when my football had gotten bigger than my basketball. So I decided to go play football. If it wasn't for Coach Harris keeping me playing football, it wouldn't have happened. I just would have walked off the field because I was going to quit. I wasn't going back. At the time I walked off the field, he didn't say nothing. He just waited to come to my house. I thought he was blowing smoke up my ass. He coached Matt Darby and Keith Goganious at Green Run High. Those guys both played in a couple of Super Bowls with the Bills. At that time I was like fifteen or sixteen. I was concerned about playing basketball, but football came so naturally to me, it was easy. When I played basketball I was athletic, but I didn't possess any one good skill. I just had all-around game.

I played against some good guys in high school, but I realized how good the basketball players were when I was at Michigan State and I scrimmaged with those guys. In high school, I played basketball against Aaron Brooks, who later became an NFL quarterback. He was good. I played against Jason Capel. But the best guy I played against in high school was Tim Thomas in an AAU tournament at the University of Delaware. He was serious. He was six-ten bringing the ball up the court. I had never seen that before. I couldn't believe it. He was six-ten, dribbling the ball up the court, and anytime he got the ball near the rim, he was dunking it. Nobody could stop him. That was like '92 or '93. I mean every time he got near the rim, *Pow!*, he punched it. I was like, man, who in the hell is this dude, man? He's probably the best player I played against in high school. I've never seen nobody do that before, at least not on the same court I was on. At that time I was only a freshman in high school. My dream was to be an NBA player and I went to all the AAU camps in Michigan, Delaware, North Carolina, and South

Carolina. I was on the traveling AAU teams. I got some letters for basketball from Georgia, Clemson, Kansas, Virginia, and Wisconsin. I didn't get any from North Carolina or Duke or Georgetown, nothing crazy. But I got some good letters, major Division I basketball.

All of a sudden I was the best receiver in the country in football and averaging nineteen points, thirteen rebounds, and six assists a game in high school basketball. I played off guard. I would go down and I could bang with the boys and get up on the glass. I could jump, I could do it all. When I was a senior, I had all these schools after me. Georgia was recruiting me for both football *and* basketball.

But I just thought, *Man, I don't have grades to do shit.* I didn't have good-enough grades to make any decision to go anywhere. I had to get a grade-point average and an SAT deal to even get looked at as far as going to school anywhere. I was walking across the gym floor one day and my coach said, "I want you to come look at this." He told me about J. J. Stokes and Westbrook and I was like, "All right, man, it's cool." Going into my senior year, he said, "You know what the SAT is?" I didn't know what that was. He told me, "You got to start studying for your SAT." I'm thinking, what for? "You got to pass it to go to college," he said. I wanted to go to college, so I had to take it. Then he told me, "You've got to get your GPA over a 2.0. Do you know what your GPA is right now?" I said no. "It's a 1.6." That was my GPA going into my senior year.

My coach then told me, "Right now the only thing you're looking at is junior college, going to a Division Two school or possibly going to a black college. If you can get your GPA up to 2.0, you can go anywhere in the country where you want to go. All of those letters you are getting, you can pick any one, anywhere you want to go." That right there sounded pretty appealing to me. I said, all right, I've got to get my shit together. At this point, I pretty much knew that I was probably going the football route. Before my senior year started, we were in two-a-days and he told me this. So he put me in tutoring. I had to drive twenty minutes away to Ocean Lake High School to get me ready to pass the SAT. School started, the first nine weeks, and I made the honor roll. I made an A, two B's, and three C's. I walked in the house and showed my mom my report card, and she thought I had made it up or something. She couldn't believe it. I mean it, she could not believe it. I could just tell how happy she was that I made the honor roll by the look on her face. That right there bumped my GPA up to exactly like a 2.0. My grades dropped a little bit during the second nine weeks and dropped a little bit more in the third nine weeks. The fourth quarter I improved a little bit, but my GPA didn't go over 2.0, it stayed the same. So now I needed like an 840 or something on the SAT to scale it up so I could qualify. I needed an 840, but I didn't pass. My first time taking the SAT was like 630 or 620 or something. Now Florida wasn't recruiting me anymore. I signed with Michigan State because they stayed with me. They said, "Hey, all you got to do is pass the SAT. You got five months to pass it." I said, "All right, cool, I'll get it." I took the ACT and I didn't pass that, either. I got like a sixteen on it. I ended up running out of time. They were like, "Go to junior college or go to prep school."

I asked, what's a prep school? They told me if I went to prep school, I wouldn't lose any eligibility. The only thing about it is it's a military school. I ain't going to military school. You can cancel that. Then they tell me my other option was to go to some community college in California. But if I go to a junior college, I'd lose eligibility. So that's what I was stuck on; I didn't want to lose my eligibility. So I had to go to military school. My coach told me it's the same one where Eddie George and Cris Carter went. It was also in Virginia and he told me I was going to have to make a whole lot of changes. He says, "It ain't going to be nothing like you've been doing now." The whole time, I was thinking, I'm staying right here. I wasn't going nowhere. But we got approved for the loan and I went. My uncle Adrian Elliott ended up taking it out for me, it was $25,000. I ended up at Fork Union Military Academy. I got there and I was in culture shock. It's a prep school in the middle of nowhere and it's all dudes.

I had to shave my head, no facial hair, wear a uniform and dress shoes, and all of that shit. I had to wear them black pants and shiny, hard shoes. I never wanted anybody in my neighborhood to see me in them clothes. So when my mom drove me up there, I wore my regular clothes in the car and then changed on the interstate. It was horrible. Hospital-type bed, you couldn't have no dust on your furniture. I just remember sitting back and watching Dré Bly and Aaron Brooks, all them guys, on TV having so much fun playing college football. I would just cry and cry. I thought I had failed. I did kick-ass playing. I made thirty-three catches for 807 yards and twelve touchdowns. The first time we played, we went up to Widener College. We drove in a family van. We got up at 4 A.M. and jumped in the van. The seats were like so tight. So we jumped out of the van, I was thinking we were staying overnight. Nope. We got out and put our pads on and played our football game. I was thinking, *We just rolled like ten hours. We're going to play a football game?* I couldn't believe it.

So we got the kickoff. The first play of the game, double slant. I caught a slant and went eighty yards, untouched, touchdown. It was like "What in the hell is going on?" A big guy like me outruns everybody? Freaked some people out. Then, in the second half, I was playing in the slot. Kevin Ward was my quarterback. He ended up playing at East Carolina. So he threw me the ball and I was probably on the thirty-yard line. He put the ball up in the air and the ball probably went sixty yards. I caught the ball on the ten-yard line. I just ran past the safety and caught it. I was like, "Ooohhh." I couldn't believe it. I came to the sideline and Coach (Tripp) Billingsley was like, "Son, you are going to be an All-American." Just like that. I thought I had failed when I went to that place. But I ripped that place to pieces when it came to playing football. We were playing against major junior college and junior varsity teams from big schools, the true freshmen who had redshirted. We played against guys from Virginia, Virginia Tech. I kicked their ass all up and down the football field. Back then I was running a 4:38 (in the forty-yard dash). I was so fast and so quick they just couldn't believe it. It wasn't even funny. I was catching stuff on the run and nobody could make a tackle. So I stayed up there, and on my first SAT I got an 820. Since I was at a prep school and it's called postgraduate, my GPA also went up. Anyway, as soon I got the score and I qualified, I was out the door. Christmas came and I was gone. I didn't even think about it.

It was brutal being there. They'd kick the door open to your room at 5:30 A.M., people standing there going, "Burress, get up!" They're all standing out there in this big field with the music playing. I'm like, "Shut the fuck up." The guy who came and kicked the door open, his name was Lieutenant Kern. I don't remember his first name, but he'd come and yell, "Get up, who do you think you are?" So I was always late, the last one to get out there, and Lieutenant Kern was yelling, "If you don't get out here, I'm going to have the whole platoon doing push-ups." I'd be in the bed like this, still laying down. "Burress, you better get out here. I'm going to put you in the bathroom detail." Fuck, I wasn't scrubbing no toilets. I had to mop the floor and scrub it. So I get up and I go outside and all my guys are in push-up position. They're on me, saying, "Come on, Plax, man, come on. Get up." So then Lieutenant Kern says, "Parade rest." They wouldn't start nothing until everybody got out there. I was in Charlie Company and all the companies would be out there. But you can't leave one guy behind. Everybody has to meet. You don't get out there, you get demerits.

I had so many demerits and I walked so many tours in those hard shoes. I'd be late, so they'd write me up. Then, after football practice, I'd walk the tours. They had this big field over here, and they had a big hill you had to walk up and down. You'd walk up and down until they got tired of seeing you walk. It would be maybe an hour. If you were messing up, probably two. Me and Lieutenant Kern were cool, but I was just undisciplined. There were kids there younger than me, they'd been going there their whole life. From elementary school, junior high, and high school. So they outranked me. They were like lieutenant colonels when they were twelve years old. So I was walking by guys thirteen or fourteen years old that I had to salute. Every time you walk by them and you see their stripes, you got to salute them. Man, I wasn't saluting no dude twelve years old. They'd yell at me, "Get over here, what's your name?" I'd be like, "Man, get the hell out of my face, twelve-year-old." I walked away, and that's the shit that would get me in trouble. You've got to salute your superior officer.

This kid was like twelve years old. I was eighteen and I said, "Man, come on, on the outside you'd get your ass beat. I'm not saluting you, that's disrespectful." I would rather walk that hill in them hard shoes than salute a twelve- or thirteen-year-old. I was young. I wasn't going to salute anybody. But the school did instill the idea of discipline in me. That was the purpose for me to go there, for later in life. Back then, though, I was so happy to get out of that place. But then I got to Michigan State and the NCAA said I wasn't eligible to play right away because the prep school is a full-year program. Michigan State didn't even know that when they pulled me out of Fork Union and told me to get there. As soon as I passed the SAT, they pulled me out of the program and I wanted out. So I had to sit out the 1997 season. But I was out of Fork Union. I took it.

School Daze: Getting a Rep

When I left Virginia to go to Michigan State, it was like another culture shock for me. I'd never been out of Virginia except one time to go to football camps in South Carolina and at the University of Florida. Florida was recruiting me way back then, but when they found out my grades made me a Prop 48—meaning I couldn't play the first year—they backed off.

Michigan State was the only place that stuck with me. But when I got to school, I was just so different. I wore like Timberland boots and nobody up north wears Timberland. The other students looked at me and said, "Where did you get those yellow boots." I'm like, "Y'all don't wear Timberland?" "No, man, we wear Rockports." And when I met with guys like Mateen Cleaves and Morris Peterson, who were on the basketball team, they used to clown on me. I remember Morris said the first time he saw me, "Who in the hell does this guy think he is?" I had my Levi's, I had my fitty hat, my baggy jeans. Everyone thought I was crazy, I just dressed so differently than how those guys dress. It was so opposite I became like a trendsetter 'cause nobody dressed like I did.

I had a vision.

I had never heard of a lot of these rappers who were big up north, like Master P. I never heard of 8Ball & MJG. Where I was from, we got more of the East Coast vibe, like Biggie and Jay-Z. Being somewhere new, it kind of opened my eyes to the world. I was just so green to the rest of the world. That's why I'm so glad I went to college. If I had just stayed back in Virginia my whole life like so many of them guys I grew up with, I never would have known any of this.

It's like the first time I went to Flint, Michigan, with Mateen, Morris, and my teammates Robaire Smith and Sedrick Irvin. It was like the first time I realized that everywhere you go got a hood. I didn't know that. I thought I was from the only hood because I never left my area. And Flint, now that was serious. It was worse than what I grew up in, so it really opened up my eyes about life. I wasn't used to every restaurant you went into having bulletproof glass.

To see something else was important to me. I guess it was one of the reasons me and Mateen formed a wonderful relationship so quickly. We were all from the same environment. But me going to college opened my eyes up to the world. I realized I knew nothing about music. I didn't listen to anything but rap. I didn't hang around white people up until that point. Dating a white girl was a cardinal sin where I grew up. It just didn't happen. I didn't have white friends unless I played with them and I didn't hang out with any of them.

And you know what is so sad, the people still there in Virginia Beach that I left, they are probably thinking the same way I used to think. That is what is so messed up about it, 'cause if you never leave, you never know. I cannot believe I almost missed out on this great opportunity to go to college. Where I grew up, you went to high school, you played ball, you didn't go to college. And then people would just tell playground stories all day. Everyone got these great playground legend stories.

When I did it, when I ended up going to college and they started seeing me on TV, some of my old friends really resented it because it was supposed to be them and not me. When I would go home, some people thought I was coming home to show off. But I come home because this is what I knew and I wanted to come back to help. It all opened my eyes to a lot of stuff both about the world and where I was from. It's like I was blind before going to college.

When I first got to Michigan State, it was kind of screwed up. I had gone to Fork Union Military Academy for half a year to get my academics in better shape. As soon as I was eligible academically, they told me to come to Michigan State, so I got there in January 1997. But then they found out that for me to come in and play right away, I had to have stayed at Fork Union the entire year. So I couldn't play football my first year there in 1997. That was messed up. I couldn't even practice with the team.

So that spring, Coach Tom Izzo let me scrimmage with the basketball team so I could stay in shape. I was a pretty good player and the guys would tell me, "Why don't you come out?" But I wasn't in that league. Those boys are really big. I could play okay, but not like that. Those guys jumped so high. Football was my thing. But I liked those guys and hung out with them a lot, so that was cool. With the football team, I could work out, but not if the other players were around. I had to do a lot of stuff on my own or work with a coach one-on-one when I could.

Anyway, I finally got myself eligible to play on the team and I was playing for Nick Saban. Nick and me didn't see eye to eye, we didn't get along too well right from the start. That fall, one of my best friends from where I grew up, Cedric Warren, got hurt playing for Florida. He was a cornerback for them and broke his neck and was out of football for nearly a year. I was worried, so

I went to Coach Saban and he said I couldn't go see him. We never really got along from then on. It was my first year of playing, so I understood it was important for me to be there. But he wouldn't let me go see my best friend in the hospital who's almost paralyzed.

Saban is a great coach and all, he's really smart and knows the game. And on the football field he is a totally different person from when he is coaching. But I didn't like him and we didn't get along well. No freshman can come into his program and talk to the media. That's his rule and that's because of me. My first year, I talked to the press a few times and I was talking shit. That's what I grew up with. That's what everybody did. It wasn't like it was some big deal, it's just how everybody talked, how everybody got up to play. That's all we did. I thought it was normal. Before we played Michigan that year, the reporters asked me how we'd do. It was a big game for us and I'm like, if our offense is doing its thing, it will be "like taking candy from a baby." I had six catches, fifty-five yards, and a touchdown and we lost, but what did people expect me to say?

Anyway, from then on, the coach had a gag order on all underclassmen. So we really weren't seeing eye to eye at that point. We had kind of a coach-player relationship, but it wasn't anything special outside of football. All of that came after the whole thing with Cedric, when he just flat-out told me no. He didn't give me no explanation or nothing. I thought, *Man, my best friend I grew up with was in the hospital almost paralyzed and I can't even go see him for a day?* That right there let me know where he stood as far as football and life and everything outside of that. We never really got along.

Anyway, I played in the '98 season. I was finally getting in there and I was playing pretty good. We were 6–6, but we were better than that. I set the school record for catches with sixty-five, had 1,013 yards, and I tied the record for touchdown catches with eight. Andre Rison held that record before me, so that was pretty cool. I was named first-team All–Big Ten. I was playing on special teams, too. I caused a couple of fumbles on special teams. I don't think I'll be doing that ever again, but I was good at it.

So we came back for the 1999 season and it was more of the same shit. Saban didn't want me talking and we just weren't gettin' along. The fourth game of the season against Iowa, we were killing them right from the start. I caught six passes, had ninety-five yards, and three touchdowns in the first quarter and he took me out for the rest of the game. I had sprained my thumb catching punts before the season opened, so I had this special tape job on my hand.

I wasn't really doing anything practically up to that fourth game against Iowa. My hand started feeling a little better, and I had that big game. The first quarter he took me out, and I was wondering, What was that all about? The Iowa players weren't very good anyway, and we wound up scoring forty points. But it was the fact that he took me out of the game and he wouldn't let me play that bothered me.

The next week we played against Michigan, and I ended up with 255 yards and a touchdown. That was a great game. I was talking that one up two weeks before the game. I was talking about Michigan before we even played Iowa, and Saban hated that.

But, man, that was the big game for us, Michigan vs. Michigan State. That's the game you circle with a red marker and put an asterisk beside it. That's a big rivalry, that's a big game. Everybody says that the rivalry is Michigan vs. Ohio State. But for us, it's Michigan. We play those games fast and physical, a lot of trash talking. The student body was sitting in front of the Spartan statue and sleeping there the whole week before the game. They put their tents up in front of the Spartan statue, guarding it from anybody from Michigan who might come down and egg it. It's cool, that whole week you're walking to class, riding your bike to class, all the kids had pitched their tents up in front of the Spartan.

For me, the big talk was about David Terrell. Everybody was saying he's the best receiver in the Big Ten. He's from Virginia, too, so people are saying he was the best receiver to come out of Virginia and all of that. We got out there on that field, man, and it was like playing on air that day. I couldn't be stopped. I remember it like it was yesterday. Then they put Terrell on me for three or four plays and I just dogged him and threw him on the ground. I jumped on him and stuck my helmet on his chest. We were out there talking trash and I told him I was the best player he was ever going to play against. Then there was the one I caught on the fly and barely hung on to it. I said, "Man, you can't cover me, I'm going to be the best player you ever play against. Don't ever forget that."

I ended up seeing him at home one time in Virginia Beach on the oceanfront or something, but we really just said, "Hey, what's up?" Not a real greeting. Anyway, I would say I'm the best wide receiver to ever come out of Virginia up to that point, and hey, I still feel like I am. The game was great. We won 34–31. I ended up with ten catches and I set the school record with 255 yards and I had a touchdown. After the game, Michigan coach Lloyd Carr said about me, "Burress was incredible. We just couldn't handle him."

The other thing about that game that was cool is that Tom Brady was playing for Michigan and he almost brought them back. We were leading 27–10 in the third quarter and he took over. He'd been splitting time with Drew Henson, but then Carr left Tom in and he went thirty of forty-one for 285 yards and a touchdown. He completed fifteen straight at one point. The dude was scary even then.

We were 6–0 and feeling pretty good. The next week we went to Purdue, and they put up thirty-five in the first half. The first drive we went down and I got a neck stinger right away—pain shooting all the way down my arm. I ended up coming back later in that drive and looking over my shoulder and got a touchdown in the back of the end zone on Michael Hawthorne. He played down in St. Louis, New Orleans, a big guy, rangy guy. They put him on me because he was big or whatever.

But then they were running the score up on us, it was 28–6 in the second quarter after Drew Brees threw four touchdown passes. It was 35–14 at halftime, something crazy like that. So we came back up and just ended up throwing the ball around, but Brees was rolling. They beat us 52–18 and Brees and Purdue wide receiver Chris Daniels went nuts. Brees was forty of fifty-seven for 509 yards and he hit Daniels twenty-one times for 301. It was ridiculous and that was the game when Coach Saban cussed out defensive end Robaire Smith on national television. That was his biggest problem. When Saban got mad or something happened, he would just spaz out, flip out. There was no in between. I couldn't believe he cursed Robaire up and down like that on national television.

Robaire gave up a big third-down play, then somebody got a penalty and then Robaire came back and got a personal foul two plays later. Saban may have called a time-out just to rip him in half. I couldn't believe it. For a guy to talk to Robaire like that. And some of the things he was saying to him, MFs and fuck you, and I was like, *Damn, this is a college coach talking to a teenager like that.* A whole lot of players on the team lost a lot of respect for Coach Saban on that one. I remember having a conversation with New York Giants cornerback Sam Madison, who played for Saban down in Miami. I was like, "Man, the one thing I didn't like about Saban . . ." and before I even got it out,

Sam said, "He don't have no people skills." I was like, "Well, shit, you already know." Saban cussed out that other kid, the defensive tackle Manny Wright, down in Miami in front of the whole team and Wright started crying.

Those are the things that he does. He shouldn't coach at the NFL level, he has to coach college ball because he's so overcontrolling as far as talking to people. You can't talk to grown men that have kids and stuff the way he wants to talk to people. So he should stay in college. He shouldn't come up to this level and talk to guys the way he would talk to them in college. He'll get his ass beat.

As that season is going on and people are talking about me and where I might go in the draft, he starts talking me down in front of the whole team, saying I'm a late first-round or early second-round pick. He's saying in front of everybody that I'm not a dominating player or I'm not a dominating blocker downfield. He was totally in my face and I was just like, "It's cool, everybody is saying I'll be a top ten pick." He says, "Well, that's not what they're telling me." However you see it. So I think that Michigan game just kind of set everything off. I just went through the roof.

But in the Purdue game, we're starting to come back. We're probably on the ten- or twelve-yard line and they call the same pass route I scored on in the first half. I'm supposed to run a fade route to the corner of the end zone, but the guy played so far outside, so I can't run the fade. I ended up taking an inside release. I had the cornerback beat to hell, beat so bad, and Bill Burke laid it up a little too high and the safety came over and intercepted it and ran for a touchdown.

I had to run it that way. The fade wasn't going to work. I came to the sideline and Saban is like, "What the fuck are you doing? You don't take an inside release on a fade. You can't do that. Who the fuck do you think you are?" There was no need for me to explain what I saw or what I was doing. I said, "Hey, the guy picked it off, I ran a great route." Saban kept fussing and so I said, "Okay, you finished? I'm going to go sit down." That was the look I had on my face. I could take it. I figured we'd try other plays for next week.

So then we went up to Wisconsin and I had five catches for seventy-five yards against them. It was my first time playing against Jamar Fletcher, who was real good in college. He was an All-American cornerback. In high school, I was just so much better than everybody, but here was the first time I felt like I was playing against a guy with skills as good as mine. It's the first time I remember me getting my antenna up.

Every time I face somebody who is considered really good, like when we played against Green Bay and Al Harris in the NFC Championship Game, or somebody who talks trash about me, that gets me going. Playing on Sunday night or Monday night, same thing. If someone says they can cover me, that I'm not big or I'm not fast, it's on. I'm not Randy Moss. I have a lot of respect for him. But I'm a beast to handle on Sunday. My thing is, I'm facing a guy one-on-one. I want to see where I fit in as a player. I want to prove something to myself.

So I'm playing against Fletcher. I was running as fast as I could. He was running as fast as he could. We were just going at it. I was giving this guy some of my best stuff and I beat him one play. Then he beat me the next play. He ended up being a first-round pick later on, but he didn't make it in the league that good. His problem was that he used to sit on every route, waiting for an interception. He knew at the college level it was hard for people to throw over the top of you all the time, so he'd wait on the short stuff and he had enough ability to recover if they threw deep. In the NFL, you can't do that. You get burned and then all of a sudden you lose your confidence.

Anyway, going into that game, our defense was giving up

only thirty-nine yards rushing a game at that point, they were number one in the nation in rush defense. Wisconsin's Ron Dayne needed like fifty-three yards to break the all-time rushing record. By the time he was done, he had 214 on thirty-four carries and it wasn't even close. We were never in the football game. We ended up losing 40–10. Then we came back home and beat Ohio State.

Then, after Ohio State, we went to Northwestern and beat the Wildcats. I had five catches, three touchdowns, 164 yards, and that just kind of sealed it. It was over.

Coach Saban heard I wasn't going to class, so he pulled me in and said, "If you don't go to class, I'm going to cut your game tickets. You're not just going to play football and go to the draft." I was like, "Hey, it doesn't matter. You were the one telling me I wasn't that good anyway." He would have people just go to my classroom and peek in the window and see if I was there in every class I went to, whatever. After the Michigan game, I just stopped going to class. I knew I was going pro. With the tickets, I'm from Virginia. My people are not coming way out here anyway. I don't have anybody to give my tickets to. Maybe my teammates. It didn't matter if he took my tickets. Nobody was coming to see me.

We ended up playing against Penn State, and T. J. Duckett had five touchdowns and Penn State triple-covered me the whole game. After we beat them, we get an invitation to play in the Citrus Bowl. We were actually in the locker room and the members of the Citrus Bowl committee said, "How would you like to go play in the Citrus Bowl?" We just went crazy! This was a New Year's Day bowl game.

About a week later, we started hearing all the stuff about Saban going to LSU. We were sitting in a meeting with him and he said straight to our faces, "I'm not going to LSU. I know you guys have been hearing about me going to LSU. I'm staying right here. I'm finishing what I started." Some of the guys got up clapping, like Josh Thornhill. Josh was a big Michigan State guy. His dad played there and then his younger brother. So he was buying what Saban was saying. Saban loved Thornhill, too. So Josh stood up clapping, I remember.

Then the next day, the very next day, Saban came in and said, "Guys, I'm going to LSU." So that let me know where he was coming from as a person and how loyal he was. He had sat down and looked his team in the face and said he wasn't leaving, then turned right back around and said, "I'm leaving." Yeah, he was the head coach. He was the head football coach and you're going to pull your team in a meeting and tell them you're not leaving, and you turn back the next day and say, "Guys, I'm going!" We were dumbfounded. He did it again, too, last year, when he said he wasn't going to leave the Dolphins, and then *boom*, he's gone to Alabama.

I didn't trust anything he said at that point. Nothing. So he's gone right then, done, on the plane. After he said that, we still had a bowl game in two and a half weeks, but now we didn't have a coach. He had already signed when he walked in and told us that. So we didn't even know who our coach was going to be. A bunch of guys went to the athletic director and said we wanted Bobby Williams to be the coach. Bobby is an intelligent coach, and he worked for Saban for twenty years or so. He was very deserving.

I remember, going into the week before the Citrus Bowl, I ended up going to a funeral over the Christmas break and I missed the trip going to Orlando. I told Coach Williams that I had to go to a funeral back home in Virginia. He let me go home when the team was at their practices. He let me go home and miss the last day of practice and travel, and the team flew to Orlando. I ended up getting there that night around nine or ten. That just let me know what he had as a coach versus Coach Saban.

We got to Orlando and everything was running smoothly. I was twenty-two and that was my first time to Orlando. The hotel we stayed in was the Pelican. It was so beautiful. We had been practicing inside the whole week in Michigan because it was so warm in Orlando. When we got to Orlando it was eighty degrees, and we were like, "Oh yes." And the first night we got there we didn't have any curfew. All we did that day was go to the stadium, take our team pictures, see the locker rooms and practice field, and all that. And then the coaches said, "Y'all are free for the night." Saban never would have done that. I would say our team got closer than they ever had been that night. Man, we tore it up—when I say "tore it up," I mean the whole city of Orlando. We tore it and we were drinking so much beer. I was sitting in Hooters and we were drinking pitcher after pitcher after pitcher. We ended up going out and we tore the place up, had so much fun, man. Woke up the next morning and everybody was hungover. Then we went to practice, but when you are twenty-one, twenty-two, you can do that. You can go out and drink beer all night.

We got in about three or three-thirty. Everything in Orlando closes at two, so we got back to the hotel early enough to get about five, six hours of sleep. It was good. Woke up, went to practice, had a great week of practice. I remember getting ready to play. We were facing Florida, and everybody was saying we were too big and too slow, and that we couldn't compete with SEC teams. Everybody was talking trash all week. Cedric, my best friend who hurt his neck, was on the Florida sideline. He had his jersey on, but he wasn't playing. I had a friend, Keith Kelsey, who played, and Eugene McCaslin, and Marquand Manuel. He was a true freshman. I would go over to the hotel and hang out with them because my best friend was over there. We would get to talking so much trash. Those Florida boys were saying, "Y'all can't beat us, we're too fast." I just said, "Okay, man."

So we got to game day and right before the game, Coach Williams was out there, and he said, "Burress, you ready?" I said, "Yeah, Coach, I'm ready, I'm always ready." He says, "Good, because I'm going to let these motherfuckers fly like the Blue Angels tonight." Coming from your head coach, him talking like that, I was like, *Holy shit.* First play of the game was a pass to me for thirteen yards. I thought, hey, he wasn't bullshitting. By the time the game ended, I had thirteen catches for 185 yards and three touchdowns. I was so physically exhausted by the time the fourth quarter hit. We hadn't played in warm weather like that all season. On running plays, I was literally walking up to the line of scrimmage. I was so exhausted. By the fourth quarter, I was so dehydrated I was squeezing sponges on my head. The game was so much more intense than the practices. I remember that I was thinking I had to pace myself for the passes. That's how bad I was. I was exhausted.

Lito Sheppard and Robert Cromartie were taking turns covering me. They talked a little bit before the game, but I was so tired by the end that I couldn't even talk to them. But that was sweet, to hear them talking like that before the game about how we didn't have the speed, we couldn't run with them. I caught every ball that came to me except one. They were covering me one-on-one the whole game and I just couldn't believe it. I remember being double- and triple-covered at Michigan State. When I got out there and looked over at Florida coach Steve Spurrier, I said, "Y'all don't have anybody. Am I going to be playing like this the whole game?" He didn't say anything. I thought, Oh my God, I cannot believe that they're treating me like this. They did not double-cover me one time the whole game. Thirteen catches later, I set a record for the Citrus Bowl. I don't know if Spurrier even remembered me from when I tore up his summer camp when I was in high school. But yeah, man, we let the motherfuckers fly. I love that.

So we got done with the bowl game, beat Florida 37–34, and I got ready to tell my mom I was going to the NFL. My mom had no idea what was going on, she was so green about the whole thing. She had no idea I was going to the NFL. She knew I was a pretty good player in college, but I only played in college for two years. So I said after the game, "Mom, I'm going into the draft." She said to me, "What you need to do is stay in school, you don't need to go to the draft." Maybe she thought I was joining the army. I said, "Mom, look, I'm going to be a top ten pick." She didn't really understand what was going on. But after the game I had $5,000 in my pocket. I was counting the money and giving it to her. She said, "Where did you get all this money?" "Mom, look, I told you I'm going to the draft. Take this money. I'll see you in a couple of days."

When I say she was green, it's not that she wasn't smart, she was just inexperienced about pro football.

"Mom, take this money, I've got to go down to Miami and see a financial adviser." She asked again, "Where did you get all this money?" I told her, please understand. I looked at my cousin and said, "Tell her what is going on." I said, "Mom, this is what is going on. I'm going into the NFL, I'm going to be like a top ten pick and this is what I'm scheduled to make." And I told her a really big dollar amount. My cousin looked at my mom and he said, "Baby, your son, he's made it." She didn't believe it and then about two days later she understood what was going on. She was just so green, it was hilarious.

After I got back from Miami, I came back home to buy my mom a car. I bought my mom a Jaguar, but I didn't give it to her right away. Then I called her and said, "Mom, this is what I want you to do, go out and find any house that you want and we will go get it." She said, "Boy, I don't have no money for a house." She didn't understand, she didn't know what was going on.

Then I came home with a Jaguar. I was staying at my best

friend's place and we planned a big IHOP breakfast for the next morning. My mom would be outside at nine o'clock and a Jaguar would be there. So she came in and said, "Whose car is that, it's nice." "Mom, it's yours." She busted out crying. She had no idea. And before we could make it out of the neighborhood, she got pulled over by the police.

After that, I told her again we needed to find her someplace to live. I told her to go find a house, and you know what she did? She got a town house. It's an upscale town house, but it's not a house. I'm like, "Mom, what are you doing, I told you to go find a house, anything you want." She said, "This is good enough for me." I said no. I wanted her to get a house with a yard and everything and she went and bought a town house in a community and moved into that. Finally, she found something that was being built and got that. She spent two or three months in the town house and then moved.

Even then, my mom never asked me for anything. I tried to give things to her and she'd say, "Why are you giving me all this stuff?" It was because I wanted to. She'd go for a while without groceries in the house, never ask me for anything. My brothers were still living with her and she would go for periods of time and not call me and not have groceries in the house. You had to give it to her, she wasn't going to ask for a thing. She wasn't like that, even though if she would ask me, these were things I never even thought twice about. Anything she wanted she could have.

Anyway, I signed with Leigh Steinberg to be my agent out of college and so I went to Irvine, California, to do my training. I was out there hanging out with Jamal Lewis and Ralph Brown. They were working out with their agent and we'd meet up at night. Every day when I was done working out, I was hopping into this Ford Explorer that my agent rented for me and we all drove to L.A. to party. Man, I was young, I was going to the NFL, and I wanted to have a good time. It's like an hour, hour and a half, each way, but I was going to have a good time. One night we got back early in the morning and I parked the truck somewhere it wasn't supposed to be. When I woke up, the truck was gone, towed or something. I don't know. I never saw that truck again. Don't know what happened to it.

I went to the NFL scouting combine in Indianapolis and I was just there to have fun. I didn't care about all this stuff, all these interviews. I was rooming with JaJuan Dawson, another wide receiver. He was a good player, but he was kind of tense, worried about doing everything right. Me, I flew a couple of girls in and we went drinking every night at one of the bars in a hotel across the street. I went to a couple of Pacers games that week, just having fun. One night I was in there and the New York Giants people came up to me and wanted me to take their personality test. That test is famous around the league because it's like three hundred or four hundred questions.

So I looked at it and I said, "You guys aren't even in the top ten, I'm not taking this." It was going to take two or three hours to do. The Giants had the number eleven overall pick in the 2000 draft and selected Ron Dayne. Years later, when the Giants signed me as a free agent, they never even mentioned it.

Anyway, I knew there were a bunch of guys who were all uptight, but I was just relaxed, having a good time. Me and Peter Warrick, who went number four overall to Cincinnati, were just chillin', no problems. All these guys were worried about meeting with these coaches and I was out there meeting with Jose Cuervo. That probably helped me get an early rep with teams, but I didn't care. I was just having fun, living it up. I went back to California after that and got ready for my Pro Day at Michigan State. The Steelers wanted to work me out the day before the Pro Day, just me, a private workout. So I flew all night to get back to Michigan, but I was dead-ass tired. I was supposed to meet with them at two in the afternoon. But I slept through it. I got a call from Coach Bill Cowher that afternoon and he said, "We missed you, what happened? I flew all the way here to see you work out." I said, "Coach, my bad, I'm just dead tired." So we met the next day before my workout and talked. I didn't care at the time and Coach Cowher was cool because he understood I was being honest with him. I told him, "I'll make it up to you and we'll do it tomorrow."

I went to my workout the next day and ran a 4:38 in the forty, so I was set. I'm six-five and I run that fast. I'm going in the top ten, I know it. So I started taking trips in April to the top teams. They all wanted to do these individual interviews. My first stop was Tampa Bay and I met with Tony Dungy. He was pretty cool, but he started showing a tape of my Citrus Bowl game against Florida, where I had like 185 yards, three touchdowns, and set the record with thirteen catches. But all he pointed out were all the plays where he said I was loafing. He's asking me, "What happened here where you were not running?" I said, "Coach, I was tired from all the running I did on my touchdowns."

The next trip I was supposed to go on was to the New York Jets, where Bill Parcells was running the team. They ended up with four first-round picks, something crazy like that. But the night before I was supposed to fly there, Michigan State won the NCAA tournament in basketball (on April 3, 2000). We beat Florida. Mateen was like the MVP of the tournament. He played great, coming back in the game with a sprained ankle when Florida was starting to rally, all that stuff. So we're partying all night long, having a good time when I realize, *Shit, I got a flight in like an hour.* I was supposed to get to the airport at 6 A.M. I had just enough time to shower and get a ride to the airport. I jumped on the plane and got to New York, flew right into LaGuardia.

So I got there and went right into see Parcells. I looked terrible and I still smelled of alcohol. He looked at me and says, "What the hell is going on with you?" I said, "Coach, look, my boys won the national championship last night and we were up all night partying." I just told him straight. He said, "All right, you're only young once, have a good time." Then we go on talking and he starts in on how all receivers, we're just like Keyshawn, we're all prima donnas and out of control. I took it like Bill was just talking to me about how all us big receivers, we want to talk trash, be brash, and make the big plays. That was the year the Jets traded Keyshawn to Tampa. So they were talking about trading up to the number four pick to get me. I knew Parcells was a great coach. He and Coughlin have the same kind of background and stuff. Parcells is a great coach and a disciplinarian coach, too. He wants it done the way he wants it done. It's his way or the highway. Play hard all the time.

So I got done with them that day, but I still haven't had any sleep. I'm tired as hell, but I had to go back to the airport to catch a flight to Baltimore. I got to LaGuardia and I was sitting there waiting for my flight. The next thing I know, my cell phone was ringing and it's Leigh Steinberg saying, "Where are you? They can't find you in Baltimore. You never showed up." I fell asleep at LaGuardia and I missed my flight. I got up and I was yelling at everybody, blaming them for letting me sleep. I then had to figure out how to get to Baltimore. I finally got like this last flight out and it was just a terrible flight. The weather was bad, it was a prop plane, we were bouncing all over the place, and they couldn't land it at first, but I finally got there. I got some sleep and then I was supposed to meet with them the next day.

So anyway, I headed over to Owings Mills, where the Ravens have their facility. Here I am talking with Ozzie Newsome. I'm finally talking with a black man and I'm thinking this is going to be great. Everything was going great, but Ozzie completely misled me. He said, "We've got the number five overall pick, and if you're there, we're taking you." I'm thinking, cool, I'm set. Well, it came to the draft and I was sitting there watching and Baltimore came up to pick. I was telling everybody, Ozzie said he's going to pick me. But what did they do? They took Jamal Lewis and I was like, What's up with that? My man lied right to my face. That's why every time I play against Baltimore, I try to give them everything they can handle. (I have thirty-five receptions for 579 yards and four touchdowns in nine career games against Baltimore.)

So anyway, Corey Simon went next to Philadelphia and then Thomas Jones went to Arizona. Here come the Steelers, the team I slept through the workout with, and they took me. I thought, that's cool. I'd never been to Pittsburgh, but I was good with it. Coach Cowher seemed cool with me. And I was a top-ten pick, just like I expected.

Starting in Steeltown

When you play in Pittsburgh, it's kind of like you're everybody's neighbor. It's not a big city. Not like New York. In New York, there are so many things to do and people recognize you for the things you do, but they don't just make it so uncomfortable that you don't want to go out of the house. In Pittsburgh, they love the Steelers and they live and die with them. They have a hockey team and the Pirates and the university, but when the Steelers don't win on Sunday, it's like the whole city is depressed.

The fans are so loyal and they're everywhere. It's funny, when I first got to New York and we'd go on the road, we'd get to the hotel and I'd say to the other guys, where is everybody? There'd be hardly any Giants fans at the hotel where we'd stay. When I was in Pittsburgh, they were everywhere. The fan base is incredible. They were all over the lobby, cheering you on, wanting to meet you. There were like three hundred or four hundred fans in the lobby. I just thought that was normal until I got to New York. When I was with Pittsburgh, you couldn't even walk downstairs in the hotel. You had to get security to walk you out the front door if you wanted to go eat.

And in the stands, it was the same. We would go to Seattle, Oakland, San Francisco, San Diego, and it was like it was a home game for us. It always seemed like it was 60 percent Steelers fans in the stands wherever we played. I didn't realize how popular Pittsburgh was as a team. The fans were crazy. That was cool, but when you got back to Pittsburgh, it's like you never had a moment of your own. The fans recognize you all the time and they're genuine about it. I couldn't have imagined it being better, but it was just so small that everybody was on top of you. It can be a rough time playing there if things aren't going good. If we lost on Sunday, the town would be sick for the whole week. The players call it the little big fishbowl.

It's also a rough town. Not as far as the media goes, but I've never seen so many homeless white people in my life. I thought the only homeless people were black until I got to Pittsburgh. I'm serious. I had never seen that. I had no idea. But it was horrible to see. It's still horrible.

For me, I never really thought I was accepted in Pittsburgh with the fan base. I just never really hit it with them. But honestly, Pittsburgh was a blessing for my career. There is no way I could have gotten drafted to New York or Miami back then. I'd probably be out of the league right now. That's how hard I was partying. I thought, Shit, I can do this my whole life. I can party and play football my whole life. I just thought that's how it was supposed to be. But when I got to Pittsburgh, there wasn't really a whole lot to do. It kind of slowed me down. I partied, but I couldn't imagine being in a big city. It would have been nonstop and I would have been done. New York, Miami, it'd have been over.

Of course people there always talked about the Party. It was my second year there and this club downtown offered to host a party if I put my name on it. Me and my boys would get in for free and get taken care of and everybody else would get charged to get in. Who's not going to do that when you're young and feeling good? After that party, I could never really do enough to get that reputation off me; it never left me.

Where I was at, it was crazy. It was always about what kind of car I was driving, where I was, and where I was going. I was driving nice cars, a Rolls, a Bentley. Where was my car parked? That's what I was doing at the time. But I never failed a drug test. I never got arrested for any of that stuff.

On November 19, 2001, a Monday night, we beat Jacksonville to make us 7–2. We ended up going 13–3 before losing to New England in the AFC Championship Game that year at home. It was halfway through my second year in the league and I had a bunch of guys lined up for my party. It was big-time. I had Jevon Kearse in town—it was his third year with Tennessee and he was dominating. Of course I invited Jerome Bettis and those guys and everybody was like, "Holy shit, I never seen anything like it." My mom was actually at the house and about forty of us were over there having a preparty before we went to the club.

My mom said be careful, don't be out there drinking and driving, and put your seat belt on. That was pretty funny 'cause we had a limo-bus to take us there. Before we went, everybody got a bottle of Cristal champagne. All my homeboys. I had a refrigerator downstairs filled with nothing but Cristal. That's how we partied. Pittsburgh was never the same after that.

So we were there at the club till about 3 A.M., everybody having a good time. We all got ready to leave, to get back on the limo-bus to go back to my house. By the time we made it out of there, it was probably almost 4 A.M. Halfway home, I got a call on my cell phone. The cops were there and they busted Gerard Warren and another guy who's a friend of mine. I was like we gotta turn the bus around and check this out. I got there and see they got my friend in the back of a police car already, so I acted like I didn't know him. The cops were searching Gerard's car and they found some weed, so they got ready to take him in. They were looking for one of Gerard's teammates, the big tight end O. J. Santiago. I didn't know what was going on with all this, but the next day I'm all over the media because two or three guys I know got in trouble. I didn't do anything wrong, but all of a sudden I was painted under that one because I know them and it was my party.

A couple of days after that, my friend called me up. He was still in jail, but he said I didn't have to worry about him. He'd be out in a couple of days and take care of it himself. He knew I didn't need the trouble. That whole incident, that kind of put a damper on me, even though all I did was host the party. Ever since that day, I just kind of got a bad rap after that. Plus, being that I got hurt my first year and didn't have that great a year, I was always getting looked at that way. But the fact is that I've never done any drugs like that. But everybody was looking at me that way. Hell, the worst thing that I could do would be to fail a drug test. Can you imagine what they would do if I ever failed a drug test? I'd be the first man to leave the team. I'd be done. I have never, ever used drugs. I don't beat my wife, I don't do drugs. I may drink a little bit here and there. I don't take steroids, you can pretty much look at me and see that.

It's like Jerome Bettis said to the media after the party: Just because a couple of guys got arrested doesn't mean that I'm the bad guy. But I guess it was all part of the reputation I had around the city. I guess the fans were looking at it like, this guy didn't do anything his first year and now we're good and he's doing this? I mean, I got hurt my first year. I had a dislocated and broken wrist. I was done in November after only getting twenty-two catches. This was after I'm the number eight pick in the draft. That year, 2001, I was playing pretty well and me and Hines Ward both had a thousand yards, the first time the Steelers have ever had two thousand-yard receivers in the same season. But my reputation was kind of made with the fans.

I loved the guys I played with, the coaches, the whole atmosphere there. It was so relaxed. You came in, you had fun, you busted your ass, and then you went home. That was the deal. I couldn't have played with a better group. My teammates were great, Coach Bill Cowher was great to me, the whole coaching staff. Then, when I left and I heard all the good things that the people with the Steelers said about me as a player and as a teammate, I was surprised. It made me feel good.

The only thing I didn't like was the system I played in. You'd be thrown one ball a quarter. That was it. If you caught four balls, you had the greatest game ever. But if one of those got batted down or you dropped one or one was thrown behind you, the quarterback gets sacked, all of a sudden you got nothing for the whole day. You didn't get another opportunity to get the ball. That was your four shots. But I never had a problem with Coach Cowher. I never had a problem with any of my coaches and I had three offensive coordinators, Kevin Gilbride my first year, then Mike Mularkey, and then Ken Whisenhunt.

I guess the closest time came in spring 2004, when I didn't go to a minicamp that was on the same weekend as Mother's Day. This is two years after my mother died, but it was still hard for me to deal with at that point. Me and my brothers would spend Mother's Day together, go out to the grave with flowers and clean it up. Do it right. So I didn't want to break our tradition. I didn't call Coach Cowher personally to tell him. I think my agent, who was Leigh Steinberg at the time, he called. I can remember Coach Cowher calling me and saying, "Kid, all you had to do was pick up the phone and call and tell me." He wasn't mad, he wasn't upset, he was just like he wanted us to have a relationship where I could pick up the phone and tell him the reason I wasn't coming instead of hearing it from my agent. Again, that's just how good Cowher is. He's very fair. I missed a mandatory minicamp and he didn't fine me. He just wanted to hear it from me, that we could have that relationship. He didn't want to hear it from somebody else and I understood exactly what he was saying. That was cool and that was the end of it.

Coach Cowher is one of my best friends. I love Coach to death. He came to my mom's funeral. Everybody thinks he is tough, and he is pretty tough on the sidelines, but he's not a tough guy that you can't talk to. He has got one of the biggest hearts and he's a players' coach. He is one of the people who you want to work hard for. He just wants you to tell him straight, don't lie to him. I would be late to meetings all the time and I told him straight, "Coach, I'm tired and I overslept." He'd tell me to go bust my ass in practice and I would and he never fined me. Not one time in the five years I was there. He was the kind of guy you didn't have to lie to.

One of the things that was tough in Pittsburgh is we were constantly changing quarterbacks. I went through four quarterbacks in five years there—Kent Graham, Ben Roethlisberger, Tommy Maddox, and Kordell Stewart. It's hard for any team to develop consistency when you have that kind of change.

And Kordell, he just wasn't an NFL quarterback. He was a good athlete, but he wasn't a guy you could drop back and play normal offense with. We would do crazy stuff like draw up quarterback sweeps with him just to take advantage of what kind of athlete he was. He was Slash, a receiver and all that, but not a quarterback. But our game plan was run, run, run, quarterback sneak. We did all these rollouts and bootlegs. It was hard. You couldn't run a real passing game. You saw it when he left Pittsburgh. He didn't play. He couldn't. It was the system we put him in that allowed him to be a quarterback in Pittsburgh.

In 2001, we went 13–3 and Kordell makes the Pro Bowl. He

was playing as good as he could play and we got to the playoffs. We get the bye that year and I was feeling good. That's the same time I meet Tiffany, so the world is going good. Then we got New England coming to town for the AFC Championship Game and we just didn't think they were very good. They got Brady at quarterback, they just got by Oakland in that snow game, and now they were coming to play us.

That's the game that really exposed Kordell. It was bad because we got behind and now he had to throw to lead us back. The Pats got a lead and we had to throw to get back in this game and New England showed that Kordell just couldn't do that. He ended up throwing two interceptions in the fourth quarter. One of them was toward me and he just way overthrew the ball on a pass you just don't throw in that situation. Never, under any circumstances. They had one defender cheating inside and another playing over the top. I looked back and I saw him throwing the ball and I thought it can't be for me. Then I realized I was the only one over there. He threw it so high, I didn't have a chance to even knock it down. He ended up with three interceptions in that game. The next season, we opened up 0–2 and that was the last we saw of Kordell. They put Tommy Maddox in there and he just took off.

Kordell took a lot of heat. A lot of people said all sorts of things about him, like about him being gay. It was like everything he did at Pittsburgh was just never good enough. It wasn't all his fault. He wasn't a real NFL quarterback, a drop-back quarterback. They gave him time to develop as a classic drop-back passer, but it just never happened. He couldn't, that wasn't his game.

And the personal stuff, it has to be tough. People were talking about him being gay. The players heard that, but we never talked about it. I don't know if Kordell is gay or not. It was none of our business. If ever we would have talked about it, it would have made everybody uncomfortable. If some player was gay, I don't think he could come out while he was still playing. It would be real hard. It would mess a team up mentally and it wouldn't be good for that person. Anyway, people are talking about that and now Kordell had to watch everything that he did. He had to watch the people that he hung around with. Just hanging out with your friends, or your boys and your cousins, all those things come to the surface. I think he just insulated himself after a while. I never saw him go out to a restaurant, I never saw him out hanging out on a Monday night with the team. He owned a rim shop and I would see him over there handling the business. But outside of that, I didn't see him out having fun. He alienated himself from the team. The other quarterbacks would all set stuff up and hang around, but never Kordell. He was totally the opposite from those guys in terms of personality.

After that season, when my mom died, a lot of things about my life changed. Like I said, when I lived in Pittsburgh, at first it was a party all the time. The car I was driving, the clothes I was wearing, and the jewelry. I refused to cut my hair. I had my braids. I had six of my homeboys from Virginia Beach. I wanted them around, but they didn't make it any better. I was not who I am today. Those guys, they've all got criminal records. I just refused to be the way that the fans wanted me to be. I was comfortable where I was at. There was nothing I couldn't do, no one could tell me anything. I was wild. The guys who were living with me, I was basically supporting all of them. When I shopped, they shopped. I treated them no differently from myself. It had been like that since I left high school. I still kept in contact with them. Those guys protected me like they were my direct family. With them around, I didn't need no security. It felt good. I slept good at night, I didn't have to worry about anything. I didn't have to worry about them stealing from me. I didn't worry about none of that until it happened. Stuff like that opened my eyes to how people really are and how I had to handle it. It really spoiled it for everybody.

Then my mom died. I was already working myself away from those guys, kind of distancing myself slowly but surely. But when my mom died, I went into my own little hole. That's when the ties went. It was hard, and they were not happy about it. I still get messages and letters from them. A lot of those guys are in jail, and then when other people from where I grew up go to jail, they see those guys and then I hear back from them. I get these letters hand-delivered to me sometimes when I'm around. Three guys who I grew up with, they're in there for attempted murder or what have you.

My mom knew these guys, too. My mom would cook for them, it wasn't like they didn't know her. After she died, the guys who were in jail would get word to me and say like, "Heard your mom died, sorry about that, sorry about your loss. Come see me, I still love you even though we're not close as we used to be." Blah, blah, blah. I wanted to, but at that point I was so far away from that, and when my mom passed away, I never turned around and went back.

A couple of them are out now and I run into them like at a car wash back home, or I run into them at the mall uptown. They understand, they don't hold any grudges toward me. They know I have a wife and a son, they know I've moved on from that. It was seven or eight years ago now. But I had to stop doing stuff with them. They did stuff that I'm not happy about. I've seen them guys pull guns and shoot at people. I've seen them beat guys with bats and things like that, but I never got into it physically as far as doing it with them. I was hanging with them back before I even went to college. It was normal. I never even thought about my career at that point, I was so much into having fun and drinking, I never even thought about it. These were my boys, and I wouldn't let football come between us. It was just us. Now it's totally different. I'm so far away from that. That turn came and it was all for the better. I look at myself and realize how painful it was, but that's how big the change has been.

When my mom passed away I went into my own shell. But I came back out because I had to be there for my brothers. If I wasn't there for them, it wouldn't have been right. They were living with my mom, so it was hard on them. I had gone to college, I was playing pro ball. I would come home when I could, and I got to the point where I didn't have to see her all the time. I would see her maybe once a month and that was good. I was growing up. But that whole off-season after she died, I basically stayed in Virginia Beach.

My mom's death had a huge impact on a lot of people. I remember sitting outside on my porch one morning, this couldn't have been more than three or four days after I buried my mom. I would come out every morning and sit on the porch. A car pulled up and one of my best friends from back when I was ten, eleven, twelve years old got out. He had just gotten out of jail and came to my mom's house. My mom knew his mom, we knew the whole family. I had heard he was selling and shooting and all type of stuff. So I ain't seen him in forever. Anyway, I didn't know if he was going to start shooting or what, I didn't know what to expect. I was just sitting there on the porch and he came up to me, and tears start coming out of his eyes. He said, "Hey, man, I ain't seen you in a long time, man, and I miss you. I love you. I'm sorry about your mom. Me and my mom cried when we heard your mom passed away." My mom's passing messed a lot of people up because it was so sad and everybody loved my mom. I could see how much it affected everybody. Even some of the grimiest people I ever knew would show me love by coming over. I was like, *damn*, now everybody knows where I live. I'll have to keep the doors locked and everything like that.

I had to take care of myself and my brothers. I had to let a lot of that stuff go. It was not hard at all at that point after I went through my mom passing away. It was very easy. It wasn't easy on them. But we'd been running in the same circles for so long that we all share the same mentality. *I'm not afraid of you, and I know you're not afraid of me.* My attitude became *I don't have to explain myself.* My mom just passed away, and if you don't respect that, then hey, we've got another problem. You just got to let it go. I know I'm letting it go. It's not hard to walk away from people like that when you are in a situation like that. I needed time to breathe. I didn't want to be around nobody. I didn't want to be around football. I wanted to be around my brothers and that was it. Tiff was around, but she personally didn't understand what I was going through. She came to my mom's funeral and she was down there and she ended up going back because she understood that I needed to be home with my family and grieve for a while.

The following spring, in May 2002, I got charged with public intoxication. I was just walking down the damn street in Virginia Beach. I got in trouble in that place more than anywhere else in the world. The cops there, they got nothing to do. They'd pull me over, check and see if my license was suspended, they just mess with me. On that night, me and some friends of mine and my brother Carlos, we came out of this bar, Hammerheads, and we were walking to our cars. The cop came up, pulled me out of the group, and told me to come here and sit down on the curb. I was like, "What did I do?" I was young and I just went off. I was yelling at the cop, cussing. This was bullshit. Then he put me in handcuffs. I didn't get a sobriety test or nothing, none of that. Ever. He sat me on the curb and then he took me down to the station. They released me after about two hours and then the charges get dismissed. I absolutely did nothing wrong. If I can't be in my own hometown and have a good time, they really got it out for me.

Then Carlos, when the cop put me in handcuffs, my brother started to push him. But this was Carlos, he wasn't going to hurt anybody. He was not a threat. They put him in handcuffs and put him in the cell with me. What do you think they charged him with? Assault and battery on a police officer. He was facing a minimum of six months to five years max. He was all of 145 pounds. So we had a lawyer, Larry Woodward, same guy who represented Michael Vick with his case last year. So we were sitting there talking and Woodward laid it out. He told my brother, "Just go in and plead guilty, man, don't even play with them. They want to make an example out of you." We went in to plead guilty and my brother got six months. Unbelievable. He got three months in jail and three months work release. Carlos served every day of his time. Here's my brother, all of six feet, 145 pounds, in jail. It was hard. When I came home, I saw him just about every day. It made me and him feel better, help him get through the time, sitting there talking through the glass.

What's so bad is that where he had to stay during the work release was five minutes from where we lived. Two months later, the officer who arrested my brother and brought me in, he got fired from the police force for bribery. We called Woodward 'cause we wanted to fight this thing, get it thrown out. But Woodward said we shouldn't. We really wanted to fight that.

Anyway, in 2002 and 2003, Tommy Maddox was the quarterback after Kordell got benched. Tommy was fun to play with. Funny as hell. He told me he was some great high school basketball player and I looked at him and said, "Get out of here." He told me he averaged like thirty points a game. I'm like, "You're joking." Anyway, Tommy liked to sling it around and we had that one great playoff game against Cleveland where we came back to win in the fourth quarter. We were in the two-minute offense the whole second half. I had blisters all over the bottoms of my feet when that game was done.

Then, in 2004, we drafted Roethlisberger and he looked pretty good in camp, but Tommy was still the starter. We won the first game and then Tommy went down in the second game, so Ben came in against Baltimore. He made a few plays, but we still lost big. I remember after that game talking to (running back) Duce Staley in the shower and he said, "Hey, man, our time is coming. Watch what happens, man, you're just going to take off." I didn't see it. I said, "Duce, get the hell out of my face, man. We got a rookie quarterback coming in. I'm in the last year of my contract. Duce, get the hell out of my face right now. We'll see." We played Miami the next week and beat them and then Cincinnati at home. We ended up thrashing them and then Cleveland. Ben made a few plays and we just never looked back and we were 15–1.

You look at Ben right now, it's still the same style that he played with his rookie year. He may have elevated the game as far as knowledge of the game itself, but he still does the same thing. He runs the ball at the right time. He doesn't really force a lot of things, and I think that's one of the things that separates him from a lot of other quarterbacks that we played with. He didn't make a lot of mistakes. He would run around, dive for the first down, or get out of the pocket and create more time for us to get open instead of throwing the ball out of bounds. Instead of going to second-and-ten, it would be second-and-five because he would just make something happen. He would just find a way to get it done. It wasn't pretty, he just knew how to win. I can play with a guy like that any day of the week.

He was never worried about the rush coming at him. He always played downfield. He was never afraid of looking at the line first, then downfield. He was always looking to get to somebody. A lot of quarterbacks don't play like that. They worry about the rush, worrying about where it's coming from and if they might get sacked. Even when the receivers took too much time to get open, he never seemed to play with that fearful mentality. It was always, "I'm just going to relax, wait for my guys to get open. If they don't get open, I'm going to make them get open or I'm going to scramble and give them more time to get open."

By 2004, I knew I was pretty much done in Pittsburgh. I knew they were going to re-sign Hines Ward and that was cool. He's a great ballplayer. He's a Pro Bowler and he's a great blocker downfield. He plays hard. When I came up for free agency, I knew they weren't going to keep me. It didn't hurt my feelings at all. At that point, Hines had three Pro Bowls and he fit that system more than I did. I was getting so much double coverage, they would tag all my plays with an *X* because I was only going to get a few calls. I was basically getting taken out of the game. I was running like four basic routes and I'd get maybe five passes a game. I was getting so much attention, I'd end up running eight or nine in-cuts a game because that's the way the offense was designed. They never had a player who played the position like me, so I would have changed how they would have had to play offense. They would have had to open things up just to get me the ball, like draw up a brand-new play to have me be part of it.

But they weren't going to change and I wasn't going to change who I was. I thought I was a big-time receiver, a big-play receiver who could go down the field and make plays. They weren't going to let me do that. Plus, they weren't going to use me in the red zone. I'm six foot five and I was thrown like four or five plays in the red zone the whole time I was in Pittsburgh. Look, the proof was in the pudding. They didn't throw me any fades, nothing. A handful of jump balls, maybe. The Steelers' game was to pound down in there, use the clock, and throw it to Hines Ward. I was cool with that. But I wanted to go. I didn't want to leave the players that I was with 'cause all of us were so close. But from my standpoint, the team was holding back my development as a player. I couldn't be the player I wanted to be 'cause of how the team was designed. We went 15–1 and I had thirty-two catches going into Week 10, when I got hurt and missed five of the last six games before the playoffs. I tore my hamstring.

Before the injury, I'd have one, two, two, then three catches every week. That's how it went all year, and I was averaging 19.8 yards per catch. So it's not like I wasn't doing anything when I got it. It's just that we'd run, run, play-action pass all the time. It wasn't going to change. So I had to move on. No hard feelings, but that's what I had to do.

Still, we went into the playoffs and we got back to the AFC Championship Game against New England again. We'd played them back in Week 7 and smashed them pretty good, 34–20. We were so confident we were going to beat those guys, it wasn't even funny. They came in there and just gave it to us. It wasn't even close: 41–27. I know that Bill Belichick is a smart coach. What he did was basically just rush two guys and drop nine into coverage. It killed us because we only had five going out, so they basically had two defenders for every receiver we sent out. If Ben ever broke out of the pocket, the defenders on the outside would just take off after him. It was like, Oh no. We were on the sidelines saying what are we going to do? Especially if we ran a third-and-eight, or a third-and-nine, they had us. They were like two steps ahead of us, and when they started doing that, we didn't have an answer for it. We were all just lost. It was pretty clever.

As far as the cheating stuff that the Patriots have been accused of, I don't want to get into all of that. Will we ever know the truth? No. I think the media spent too much time on it. It's not even really important, I don't think. Nobody will ever tell the truth anyway, not unless they got caught red-handed.

The funny thing is the next day after the AFC Championship Game, it's kind of like the whole city wanted to blame the game on me. On a possible touchdown pass over my head, I had Asante Samuel underneath me and got a hand on it. I ended up bobbling it and it went through my hands. They acted like they wanted to blame the whole game on me. I was like, Wow, TV, newspapers, radio, everything. The game wasn't even that close, but that one play was supposed to have been the whole reason we lost. I thought, You know what, it's time for me to go somewhere else and start fresh.

So the next season, I was in New York and the Steelers came back and won the Super Bowl. That was great for those guys. I loved it, no hard feelings. None at all. I was happy for so many guys, especially Jerome Bettis. He got to end it in Detroit, where it all started. He went home to finally win his title.

I probably learned more from Jerome than I learned from any other player I played with. From just being around him in the locker room and seeing the way he carried himself, and how much respect people had for him off the football field. I saw how people looked at him when they saw him out in public. They just listened to him. Just being around him, he's so outgoing. He's always got a smile on his face. I've never seen Jerome come to work in a bad mood. In the five years I was there, we could get whupped up on the day before, it would be Monday and I would never see him come in in a bad mood. I've never been around anybody like that. You could always walk up to him and talk to him. He'd just stay so open to you. The first time I walked into the stadium, I was in there doing an interview my first time in Pittsburgh after I got drafted. I saw him in the hallway. I'd never even met Jerome, all I did was see him on

TV, and I knew him as the Bus. He pulled me aside and said, "Hey, man, how are you doing? Pleasure to meet you. If you're looking for somewhere to stay, I've got a couple spots and I'll take you over there tomorrow so you can look at them." That's the first thing he said to me: "I'm willing to help you with whatever you need. Just tell me what you need, and I'm going to help you out, and I'll do it for you." That's how he is.

As a player, Jerome Bettis was like an animal. He was like in his seventh or eighth year and I loved to watch him. A lot of people just got run all the way over by him and he would never stop running. I couldn't imagine him coming through the hole untouched, coming down the barrel on a free safety. Ooooh, that's gotta be scary for that safety. I've just seen guys get out of the way. Some guys would get, *boom*, run over and slapped right on their back, that dude was so low to the ground. You would see him and I don't understand how this guy is a running back. He had a belly, and when he moved, everything would jiggle. But I've never seen a big guy with so much quickness. For a guy like 260 or 270 pounds, I've never seen a guy's feet so good. You'd get in the hole and guys would brace themselves because they were going to get run over and he would fake them out. He would leave them standing there. You'd be like, *Damn, did you just see that?* That was one thing he loved, making little guys miss. You couldn't tell him he wasn't Eric Metcalf or something, 'cause when those little guys miss, he hung his hat on that. If he could make a guy like 200 pounds, or somebody like 180 or 185 who he had almost a hundred pounds on miss, oh man. You couldn't tell him nothing after that. He'd say, "Did you see that move?" He'd talk all week about it.

From a class standpoint, I miss playing with him. He was always there for you and it didn't matter what it was. It was always in your best interest. He always looked out for you. I can't say enough about him. I'm still in contact with him. It hit me when I was on a plane coming back from Arizona after the Super Bowl and he said to me, "Don't that shit feel good?" I said, "Man, it's one of the best feelings in the world."

He told me that going into his last year, when he won it, he was thinking he was going to end his career without winning a ring. "I'm a Hall of Famer, it's cool, but I didn't get to the Super Bowl," is what he said he figured. After they won it, he was like, "Man, I don't think I could have ended my career and not won one, with how good it feels now. I needed it." It was his time to step away. I remember him being so beat up, his knees and ankles and toes. Jerome usually got a ten-minute tape job. You'd better get your ankles and stuff taped before he got on the table, if you were going to practice, or you might be late waiting on him. He got to have his toes taped, ankles taped all the way up to here. Then he got to get that mesh tape and I'd say, "Damn, man, we're playing football, we're not going to war." He would take so long to get taped up. He would get so banged up, he would run so hard, and he would very rarely practice on Wednesdays. It would have been on Thursdays and maybe Friday before he would be able to go. It didn't bother me or anybody else because everybody knew how passionate he was and how he ran. Nobody could be taking them hits and taking that pounding that he was taking for all those years. If somebody hit on him, he would still be running. People would be jumping on him, *boom, boom, boom.* He took a pounding and beating for the five years I was in Pittsburgh.

That was just so sweet when he won it. I was so happy for him. He called me after the game and told me how sweet it felt. Now I know what he means.

Give Me the Big Stage

My time in Pittsburgh was done. Not that I didn't love the guys I played with, but it was obvious they were going to sign Hines Ward. If they did sign him, then it was obvious they would never use me the way I should be used. It wasn't their style of play. I loved the guys, I loved playing for Coach Cowher, but it wasn't going to go on. So be it.

I had just hired Mike Harrison as my agent when my free agency began. My first visit was to the Giants. It was the beginning of March and I was the top receiver on the market. We had a great meeting. I went in and met with Ernie Accorsi, who was the general manager then. That was great. I met with Jerry Reese, Ernie's assistant. They brought Tiki Barber there to tell me what it was like to play in New York, the whole thing.

I went to dinner with Ernie and he was great. But when we get to talking about money, I didn't like what they were trying to offer me, so I left and I flew to Minnesota. Minnesota was trying to offer me a one-year $4.5 million deal and that was not going to work, either. Plus, I didn't want to go up there and be in the shadow of Randy Moss, who had just been traded to

Oakland on March 2. I didn't want to deal with being compared to Randy and all that. I've always said to everybody, Mossy is the best receiver in the league since I've been around to see.

As it turns out, I was pretty lucky, too, because that was the season where Dante Culpepper tore up his knee and was out for the rest of the year. I would have been up there on a one-year deal trying to prove myself with a backup quarterback. That's not good.

The other team that was interested in me at the time was Philadelphia, but I wasn't going to go there to play with Terrell Owens. That's just someone I didn't want to play with from what I saw of him. I'd already kind of dealt with being behind somebody else. I thought I deserved my chance to go out there and be a number one receiver. That was my whole goal. Nobody really thought I could play up until that point.

After the Minnesota trip I came back to Miami, where I was living, and it basically came down to what I thought I wanted. I did a lot of thinking and, you know what, I wanted to play in New York, the media capital of the world. I was going to take what they offered me and show them how good I am.

The tough part was that Ernie Accorsi had sort of gotten into it with my agent, Mike Harrison. After they met and we couldn't work out a deal, Ernie put out a statement that the Giants weren't interested in me at any price anymore. Later, when I read that book about Ernie, *The GM* by Tom Callahan, he said he meant it. It wasn't some negotiating ploy or anything. Back then, I just didn't think that Mike Harrison was being honest with me about everything that was being said. I was his first big client and I think he was trying to use me to make a name for himself. So I fired Mike and went with Drew Rosenhaus.

I met Drew a long time ago. When I came out of college, I met Drew. I didn't hire him then, but I figured I needed a big-time agent at this point and Drew had done hundreds of deals. I know what a lot of the media says about Drew and how people look at him, but I love him. How can you not like a guy who is going to bend over backward for you, bust his ass for you and work hard, and tell it to you straight. He gets the job done—if you have somebody who works for you and they are going out and doing all they can for you, how can you not like him as an employee? He has something like ninety clients and he calls me three or four times a week. He just calls to check in with me, make sure everything is all good.

Watching him work is ridiculous. He'll be driving a car, but he's never really driving. Him and his brother Jason are switching back phones all the time, double-checking with guys. It'll be like, "Jeremy, what's up? Where you at? Hey, we're going to lunch over here, why don't you join us." Then he hangs up and it's, "Hey, Mike, you feeling good? You working out? Excellent, big man. Keep it going." Then it's, "What's up, Dan, how are the kids?" He knows everything about every one of his clients. He just don't stop, man, he is constantly on.

Anyway, Drew worked it out with the Giants and I went back up there. I was way underpaid on my contract. We got an $8 million signing bonus. It was like my rookie deal, it was like I played on two rookie deals. My last year in Pittsburgh, I played nine games. I tore my hamstring and I had thirty-five catches for around seven hundred yards and seven touchdowns. That's in just over half a season. I was averaging twenty yards a catch and the Giants and these other teams were putting me in a category with Derrick Mason. So I was like, "Wow, that's what you think of me?" I was a free agent, but those guys like Mason got released and signed with other teams before I could get in the market, so I didn't have a lot of choices. It was just me out there, but nobody needed a receiver, so I made the best of it. I knew I could play.

I went back up to New York to meet with them again. I was sitting in Jerry Reese's office and I said, "Nobody thinks I can play." He said to me, "Well, you got a chance to prove them wrong now." That's why I wear "17." I signed with the Giants on March 17 and that will be the day of one of the greatest signings in NFL history. Three years in and I already got my championship. I just go under the radar in terms of the public.

What's important was that my team noticed. It's like what Reese said about me after the Super Bowl. He said: "This guy is passionate about football and he's a very good teammate. He's extremely competitive, he likes a challenge. All you have to do is get in his face a little bit, say something, and he's motivated. If he's playing against a Pro Bowl cornerback, one of those shutdown guys, his teammates only have to say a couple of words to him about how he's going to get shut down and he's ready. He likes a challenge and he likes the bright lights. He likes Monday night, Sunday night, big games. He doesn't want to just face any old guys. He wants the best guy the other team has. He wants the matchup guy, you know, the guy who matches up with the best receivers. You saw that with Al Harris in the Green Bay playoff game [the NFC Championship Game, when I had eleven catches for 154 yards]. Harris is supposed to be one of the best shutdown corners in the game and you saw what happened. Like I say, he loves a challenge."

But the biggest thing that sold me on playing for the Giants was Ernie Accorsi. I had asked Jacksonville running back Fred Taylor about playing for Tom Coughlin, about all the rules and how he was as a coach. Fred laid it out, said there were going to be some rules I wasn't going to like, but Fred said he was a good coach. All that stuff about the rules with Coughlin, that never scared me from going there, not at all. Ernie was the whole reason why I became a New York Giant. It's funny, the author of

The GM put a chapter in his book about me: Chapter 4, "Plaxico." I went out and read it. Ernie said some really nice things about me, which is cool.

When I met Ernie, I was like, "Damn, there are some true honest people in this business," and he was the only one up to that point that I could say that about as far as being in the front office. I'm not talking about coaches, I'm talking about being in the front office. Here is a guy who I'd never met and he studied me playing in Pittsburgh so much that he could just tell me everything about myself. What I needed to do, what I was good at, what I wasn't good at. He just shot it to me straight. He was like: "Pittsburgh didn't use you right. They didn't throw to you enough in the red zone. They didn't give you enough opportunity to make plays down the field. I thought you underachieved because they didn't use you right. If we can get you here, get you opportunities, you'll make big plays and take the pressure off our quarterback."

I was looking at him like, "Are you for real? Am I on *Candid Camera?*" From a player's standpoint, if they had the GM talking to them like that, you would have to go into a situation like that. To have a general manager say exactly what another team wasn't doing with me was amazing. I didn't feel like I had to sell myself because he already knew everything.

He talked to the Rooneys, the owners of the Pittsburgh Steelers, to ask them what type of person I was, what kind of team guy was I in the locker room. Surprisingly, Mr. Rooney had all good things to say about me. I didn't know they felt like that. Coach Ken Whisenhunt, Dan Rooney Jr.—I was surprised that they had good things to say about me as a person.

Coming from Ernie, I knew he wasn't making it up. Some people say things to you with a straight face and it's a flat-out lie. When I came out to New York, it didn't feel like a job interview. It just felt like I was sitting with someone who was genuine, loyal. I could say anything I wanted to him. I felt like I was wanted. I was sitting there and I had on a New York Yankees jacket, some jeans, some boots, and a Nike fitted hat. But that's how Ernie made me feel after I had met him just one time. He didn't make me feel like I had to put on a suit or a mock turtleneck. I felt like I was meeting with someone I had known for years. Coach Tim Lewis, then the Giants defensive coordinator and who had been in Pittsburgh on the coaching staff, told Ernie, "Yeah, you know when I was in Pittsburgh, I couldn't cover the guy in practice." He said they had to double-cover me in practice just to control me.

Ernie told that to Tom Coughlin and Tom wasn't really sold on me. He told Ernie I was big and slow. But I remember after they signed me, people asked Ernie questions. They asked, "Why would you sign Plaxico?" I was still known mostly for my rep from Pittsburgh. Ernie said, "Because I know he is a hard worker. I know he is not on South Beach chasing ass with a Bud in his hand." This is a person who has never had a bad thing to say about me.

And Ernie is like so smart about sports. If he went on *Jeopardy!* and it was all sports trivia, he's winning it. We were out at a restaurant when I came to visit and some of the waiters came up and said, "Ernie, who was the American League Triple Crown winner in 1950-whatever?" He knew it right away. He is a real smart guy when it comes to knowing his stuff. Everything he said about me in that book was right on. He said he told Tom, "Don't try to change him, let him be himself. This is not Holy Cross University." But I made the best of it. If I'm as good as I think I am, if I'm going to play like I know I can play in this market, the sky is the limit.

Eli Manning hadn't even really started yet. He was still a rookie, basically. I didn't meet with him when I visited. I just watched the tape, but I didn't get a chance to talk to Eli. From what I saw when he was a rookie, I thought he played pretty good. I didn't right then think he was a great quarterback, but how many quarterbacks are great that early? He only played half a season. I know myself from my rookie year to my third year, I just kept getting better and better and better. That is what I expected from him, that he would just keep getting better over time, and he has done it. I didn't just say no, I don't want to play with him because he's not great or as good as anybody else right now.

Amani Toomer is a great dude. I love him. He's the leading receiver in Giants history, but he didn't show any animosity toward me when I got there. Sometimes, when a player comes in and takes away opportunities from an established veteran guy, it can be hard. Sometimes it's hard for a player to accept that he's going from being the number one guy. But Amani was never worried or upset. He introduced himself. He's not selfish. Since I got there, we've had so much fun and we've laughed so much. There's never been any jealousy toward each other's success. What he does or what I do, we want to see each other succeed.

That is very rare in this business because I'm playing with guys who want glory and want passes. We want to score touchdowns. But we want everybody to do well. I don't want to play with people that are selfish. I want to play with people who like to see other people do well. I tell my guys, the receivers, every Sunday morning before the game when we meet up, "Hey, guys, we're going out there and play fast and physical. We're going to have fun. We're going to play with smiles on our faces and celebrate each other's success." I say that week in and week out. When you have guys who go out and play hard for one another, it's great. I catch a ball and Amani will come thirty or forty yards and block for me. He wants me to do well.

It's a trickle-down effect for everyone. We have receivers

who throw big blocks and make big plays. We're always the first one to celebrate one another's success and I think that it means a lot. Guys will do whatever they have to do to help one another win and there is no better attitude to have as a receiver.

The one guy I did meet with was Tiki. It's funny how people think Tiki didn't like Tom at all. Tiki was one of the guys who convinced me to come to New York. He told me how good he thought we could be if I came. What he really told me was what it was like to play in New York, under the big lights, on the big stage. Tiki said all the fans want you to do is give your best effort. He said, "When I had those fumble problems a few years ago, they tried to run me out of here. But I stayed strong and it made me a better player."

He said that, but I didn't really understand it until I played my first game. In Pittsburgh, like I said, the fans were more like the people from the neighborhood. In New York, it's a lot different. They don't really give you a chance to mess up. They're going to let you know on the first one. It's a different place to play, man, you can really tell.

You go out and play hard for a city, for a team, like that. You can really feel that spirit. The fans will really appreciate you if you play well. They come up and you can just tell from the way they shake your hand. You can really tell that they are genuine and they're really into Giants football. Nobody expected the reception we got when we got home from the Super Bowl. I didn't know how crazy these Giants fans were until we won the championship. Now that we did this, they are going to expect more, everyone knows that they are going to expect more.

In 2005, my first year there, we were playing Philly at home. I was in the middle of my best game so far, six catches, 113 yards, and a touchdown, and we won by ten. But I caught this sixty-yard pass for a touchdown, made a great play to jump over double coverage and run into the end zone. But the play got called back by a flag on the other side. It was a great play, but it got called back. So the next play, I beat Sheldon Brown so bad off the line that I ran a go route, which is what we're supposed to do if I beat the guy that bad. Eli didn't expect me to do that, so he double-pumped and he threw it up and I did one of these moves on the sideline. I dove for the ball and caught it for like a fifty-yard gain. But they reviewed it and I only got one foot down, so that got called back. The fans were booing the referees, but they didn't boo me on that one.

On the next play, I ran a skinny post. Eli threw it a little high and I jumped up in the air and the ball went through my hands. I really got fooled by the ball. I heard it right away, "BOOOOOOOOO." It was just coming down on me. I was thinking, *These boys aren't playing, they mean it.* I was like, *Damn, that's messed up. Can you believe that? They boo me over that after I almost make two great plays and I'm having a big game.* But it let me know they don't expect mediocrity. They want greatness every time.

With the way I run, because it's smooth and I have such a long, graceful stride, sometimes I just make things look like I ain't trying hard. Then I hear, "BOOOOOO." They let me know that I got to make sure I'm on my game. You can't let your mind waver. Not everyone is mentally strong enough to handle it. Sometimes you make a mistake and it affects the rest of the game in this town. They'll boo me in a heartbeat, but that's okay. It's cool. They want me to be great and I want that, too. When they booed me, I wasn't mad, I was just like, Damn, this is a tough place.

I'm not like Jeremy Shockey. If he gets booed, it's like, "This place pisses me off." That's not really how he feels. He cares; it's just how he deals with it. He gets really fired up and he's really tough and he starts trying to break every tackle, but that's when he gets hurt. I love Shock and I tell him, "Hey, man, just go down sometimes. You don't have to break every tackle." Then he says, "Fuck that, I want some touchdowns." I want touchdowns, too, but it's all right to go down sometimes. Everyone knows how tough you are. He plays through pain. I played through pain, too. But he put himself in some situations where he got hurt and he didn't have to. You got a guy at the bottom with an arm around your leg, holding you up and all of a sudden you're taking shots. The linebackers and the safeties see that and they're coming as hard as they can to take you out.

There is a difference. You play in pain, but you don't put yourself out there like that. I call it making a smart business decision. Just go down. One or two more yards ain't going to make a difference. My teammates just laugh. I'm not going to go out and try to break tackles and put myself in situations where I'm going to hurt myself trying to get an extra yard on a play that's not going to make a difference. You gotta be able to get up and make the next play. It's been working for me for a long time.

I'm not going to catch a short slant route or a little out and run eighty yards. It's not going to happen. The guys in the league are just too good, especially when you have contact made. You will pump your legs for a few seconds to see if they wrapped you up.

But if you have a guy with his arms around you, you can't move and you're just hopping around, the guys on defense are just coming in and that's what they look for. They are going to hurt you.

That five yards turning into a fifty-yard play, I did it one time and it shocked the world. I got a five-yard route against Andre Dyson this season. I just turned around, squared him up, gave him a move, and it froze him. I gave him a stiff arm and went fifty-three yards for a touchdown. But that don't happen much, and when you are in the middle of the field and you know you can't go any more, that is when players will try to hurt you. Get what you can get and don't try to be a hero on every play.

Jeremy hasn't learned that yet. He's a hardheaded man, but he'll learn. That's why he keeps getting all these injuries like a broken leg and a messed-up ankle so bad that he can't play. The funny part is that I think he's going to use this whole last season as great motivation. He's my best friend on the team and I know he's going to come back better than ever to prove all those people wrong who say we only got better and won after he left. That wasn't the reason. We got better because Eli really started clicking. We're a better team with Jeremy. He just has to stay healthy and be smart.

Like I said, you gotta make a smart business decision.

She Thought I Was a Drug Dealer

7

I met my wife, Tiffany, one night when I was out in Pittsburgh. She was having drinks with her friends. She had just passed the Pennsylvania bar exam. It was at the end of the 2001 season, the bye week before the playoff game when we played Baltimore. She wouldn't give me her number, so I gave her mine. She called me two weeks later as I was walking through the airport in Atlanta on my way back to Pittsburgh. We had just had a party in Atlanta. It was for Lethon Flowers. Good 'ol Lethon. We all went there for the weekend. It was Sunday night, eight o'clock, when she called for the first time. It was wonderful.

I was just amazed by her. I didn't know they made them like that in Pennsylvania. She was smart, really sharp, with beautiful skin. She went to Penn State and then Duquesne Law School. When we went out for the first time she drove a red Mitsubishi Eclipse. Man, that was a while ago. So we went out and I just explained to her how I grew up, where I grew up, how I was raised. She was like, "No one grew up like that." She couldn't believe it. We came from two totally different backgrounds. Her mother and father, they've been married for thirty-some, maybe forty years now. She grew up in a wonderful home. Me, I didn't know my father until I was a freshman in college. I didn't know who my father was. I guess it's like they say, opposites attract.

She grew up in New Kensington, Pennsylvania. I call her town Mayberry. Everyone in her whole town knows her whole family, and she was everything: prom queen, swimming champion, track and field. Her brother was a quarterback, she got a scholarship. We went out and she was someone I could talk to for like two hours, nonstop. We could talk about anything. So I told her how I grew up and she just couldn't believe it. We didn't grow up the same, that is for sure. Our first date was at Red Lobster. Had two tequila sunrises, it was nice. But she didn't know who I was. Actually, she thought I was a drug dealer. That was funny. Here I am, this young black guy with all this jewelry. I drove this really nice car. She just didn't know and I didn't tell her right away.

She didn't find out until after the AFC Championship Game when we lost to New England. I remember this vividly; she called me and it couldn't have been but two hours after we'd lost to the Patriots and couldn't go to the Super Bowl. Here we had a home game and lost it and I was really upset. She called and I said, "Don't call me no more." It was just because I was so upset. So she got upset and called back and said, "Why did you hang the phone up on me?" I said because we had just lost and we weren't going to the Super Bowl. She said, "What do you do?" That's when I told her that I play football. That first date, I didn't tell her at all. Never said a word. I told her my name, how I grew up, the whole story. Where I went to college, all that. I never told her what I did. I called her house one time and her father answered. He said, "Why is Plaxico Burress calling you? He is not for you." Her dad said I was running wild.

We'd been dating for about two years before I asked her to marry me. It was February 13, 2004. She was just sitting on the bed, putting her socks on one afternoon when I asked her. We were up in Pittsburgh. I already had the ring made for about three months, I'd just been waiting for the right time to give it to her. So I got the ring and got down on one knee. Then when I told her how long I had it, she said, "Why did you wait so long to give it to me?" I was just waiting for the perfect time to do it. I don't know why that time was right, but it just seemed perfect. She had no idea it was coming or nothing. I had the ring hidden in the house. It just hit me all of a sudden to do it then, and I just did it.

As soon as I asked her, she got on the phone and called everybody she knew. She was crying, hand over the mouth, just ecstatic, happy. After Tiffany said yes, everything just fell into place. It was a couple of years after my mom had passed away, so I had gotten over that. I'd just had the best season of my career in 2003 and now Tiffany said yes. It seemed like everything was just going the right way. We got married in 2005 in Nassau. It was a really small wedding, only like fourteen people. My brothers, Fred Taylor and his wife, and two of my friends from home. She had her mom, dad, sister, brother, and four of her girls from college. We kept it short and sweet. I wish my mom had been there for it. Tiffany and my mom are both very smart, but they're two totally different women. Tiffany is more book smart, really intelligent. There's not too many things that get by her or that she doesn't know the answer to as far as education and things like that. Great morals, great values, wonderful personality, she's always happy. She loves me to death, that's for sure. My mom was smart, but I think she just was more of a wise person who understood people right away. Maybe you'd call it street smarts, but it was more than that.

My wife is in corporate law. She's thinking of moving to

New York full-time. She's certified in both New Jersey and New York. That's an amazing story right there. She took the bar exam one day in New York and then the next day jumped in the car and took it in New Jersey and passed both of them on the first try. When she was going to law school, she'd do stuff like that all the time. We'd go to the store and buy her some book, she'd read it overnight and be done with it. And then remember all that stuff. Her brain capacity is amazing. She could retain all of that stuff. She could probably read the phone book overnight and remember it. She's like that with arguments. I don't win too many because she's always coming up with something. Or she'll remember something I said from three weeks ago. I don't even try to argue with her. But the best thing about her was the way she grew up, her family, her values. When I saw how she grew up, I thought it was like a joke, but it was real and it's something I want for my son.

Still, the idea of moving to New York full-time, that's a struggle. I don't want to live year-round in the city where I play. I want to get away. My house in Florida, it's my sanctuary. I had it built before we were married. She thinks it's a bachelor pad, but that's not it. I just want to get away, chill out in the off-season. It's probably a battle I'm going to lose. She's like me when it comes to her work. She wants to be the best out there. She wants to own her own law firm. She doesn't work for anybody but herself. She wants to be the best-known female attorney; she's after those types of accolades. There are things that I want for myself like that in football. I want to be the best. She doesn't want to be known as just a beautiful attorney getting by on her looks. She wants to be her own thing, and I'll support her if that's what she wants to do. I tell her to get after it. That's what you work for. But when my work is over I want to get away. I gotta rest. Her work never stops

But the way she grew up, that's what I want for our child. I mean, the way I grew up, a single-parent home was accepted. It was just the way it was for just about everybody I knew. I didn't know if having a father or daddy was supposed to mean something. I grew up in a single-parent community. I just thought that was the way life was supposed to be until I got to college. When I got to college I saw mothers and fathers and families coming to the game. I was like, man, that's nice. I said to myself I would never do to my son what my father did to me. I want what's best for my son and that's to have both his parents around.

I also saw my teammates and my friends go through the same thing that they grew up with. All of a sudden you got mother, babies, child support. They're just repeating the same thing. Guys go through a depression over it and that happens a lot because that's all they knew. That's what they went through as kids and they're doing it now as adults.

That is the way the NFL is. I would say 60 percent of the guys are like that. They grew up in it and then repeat the process of what they went through. But now it costs them a lot more. I listen to the stories from guys and I just know it's not something I want to be a part of. Some of these cats actually took care of the kids, would have them come to the games and be with them as much as they could, but the mothers are still taking them to court just to get more because of the salary they made.

There are guys writing checks for $5,000 or $10,000 a month. The mothers can get really selfish and keep coming back for more and more. All of a sudden a guy is making $120,000 per game and the mothers come back and want $30,000 or $40,000 a month. They want more and more, so it all just becomes about the money. Guys say to me, "Don't do like me." I know someone who pays about $50,000 a week of his salary over the seventeen weeks of the season for child support. He's got five kids, but still, can you believe that? That's unbelievable. That is just sickening. I would say he's making like $80,000 or $90,000 a week after taxes. It's just killing him. You should just see the look on his face every week. He's able to spend time with his kids a little, but that look on his face is bad.

Like I said, I hear the stories and I know what I went through as a kid and I just said to myself all the time that I was going to do it the right way when I became a father. Now this is what I have. I've got a beautiful wife, a beautiful son. This is how I want him to grow up. I want him in this life.

It's hard enough during the season just being away as much as I am working. I miss four days a week with Elijah. Elijah was born January 13, 2007, a week after the Philadelphia playoff game. I'm glad he wasn't born on a game day because I couldn't imagine myself playing football when my son was being born. I wouldn't have been there for the game. No way. Nothing else at that time mattered to me. I don't even look at football the same way. I look at it as this is what I have to do to provide for him and my wife. It's the best temporary job I'm ever going to have. I think with him being born it kind of made me even more re-laxed and even more patient 'cause you have to have a lot of patience when you are dealing with a child. He made me look at a lot of things differently.

He's my first child and everyone was telling me how good the feeling was. They were right. Nothing else compares. When he was born I wouldn't let anyone take him out of my sight. I was making sure that everything they said they were going to do they did and I was there when they did it. I cut the umbilical cord. I was there for the circumcision. I was there when they gave him a bath. I was there when they injected him with boos-ters.

I was there for everything. You were not going to take him out of my sight and tell me what you did to him. I was not going to play that. A lot of crazy shit can happen at hospitals, switching out babies and doing all sorts of crazy stuff. I didn't care if they thought I was crazy, they were not going to take him out of my sight. And they thought I *was* crazy, man.

I stayed in that hospital for five days. Tiffany had to have an emergency C-section, so I stayed the whole time. I ate those nasty eggs that they had at the hospital. All that food was nasty. The best thing they had there was the coffee roll, but the coffee wasn't that good.

I think the biggest thing that happened when they pulled him out was I started thinking, Man, this little dude is breathing oxygen. Feeling his heart beat, counting his ten toes and ten fingers. I was amazed that something so small could have life. It messed me up good. I couldn't believe it. I watched it, I watched life happen. It did something to me as a person. Life is so fragile, man. Something that small, breathing and moving, and you know, damn, that's my kid. I helped bring him into this world. That was the crazy part.

It was the first time I'd been around something like that and I was thinking, Man, I've got to make some changes, I got to raise this boy right. I want him to respect people.

I want him to be better than me. Not from a football, money, or success angle. I want him to be better just as a person.

That is one of the reasons I didn't name him after me. I want him to have his own identity. I didn't want everywhere he goes people be talking about me. "Your dad was a wide receiver, blah, blah, blah." The last name might give it away anyway, but I want him to have his own identity. I was talking to LaVar Arrington and he was like, "Man, you got to name him Plaxico." No, man, I want him to have his own identity.

Of course, when I told Eli Manning my son's name, he put his arms up in the air thinking I named my son after him. I'm like, "Dude, stop trippin'." Their names aren't even spelled the same. My son is Elijah. Eli is Elisha. Yeah, Eli even had a Sharpie with his name on it. He gave me one to keep for my son. Some guys get Sharpies with their names on them. So he gave me a Sharpie with his name on it and I was like, "Man, just make sure that's not even spelled this way." He said, "Come on, P Money." That's what he called me, P Money. Then again, there's probably going to be a lot of kids named after Eli Manning by the time it's all over in New York. Probably are a few already after the playoffs and that Super Bowl.

I was named after my uncle, my mom's older brother. He lives in Woodbridge, Virginia. He did a couple of tours in Vietnam, three maybe. He came out unscathed. He's not a real talkative guy, not real talkative at all. He is not going to sit down and start talking to you out of the blue. He has a wife and two daughters and he's outgoing to us, but with most people he is real quiet. From what I was told, Plaxico is some African name that means "priceless one beyond praise."

When I was a kid, people used to make fun of my name. They'd call me Mexico, Texaco. But you know what, when I got to high school I really loved my name. It was unique. If you heard my name you knew it was me, I was the only one you knew about with that name.

There is really only one. The other cool thing is that when I was in college, this man sent me a letter and asked if Plaxico Burress was my father. I picked up the phone and called him and told him no, that's my uncle. It turns out that the guy was roommates with my uncle in Vietnam and they were reunited. They got a chance to talk after all those years, so that was good.

Anyway, my big thing is to make sure Elijah is his own person. He makes me so happy. Two or three weeks after he was born, we went to the Giants office and I just went to show him off. I saw what GM Jerry Reese said about me after Elijah was born: "I think that helped him. You talk about becoming a parent, being really proud of something, he was as proud a father as you'll see when he brought Elijah in here. He took him into almost every office in the building. I think it did give him a different perspective. He has a little person he's responsible for now and that changes a person's outlook on life."

He's right, that's how I look at it with Elijah. I just want so much for him. He's the perfect child and I want him to know I did it the right way. I want to give him all that stuff I didn't get from my father. That's something I'm dealing with now. My father is Lawrence Davis. He lives in Maryland now. He called me during the 2007 season. I haven't called him yet and I don't know if I will. I don't know how much I want to say to him, what I want to say to him. I don't know if I want to talk to him at all. Pride is a tough thing.

I guess that's where I'm at now. I'd surely like to be in contact with him. At the same time, I can't pick up that phone and call him right now. I'm having a really hard time getting past that. I want to speak with him, but I also want him to feel what I went through. I'm playing ball now, I'm having success. He knows that he has a grandson and I know it pains him so much for me not ever to have contact with him. I haven't spoken to him in like four or five years and I kind of do it on purpose because I want him to feel what he put me through as a child.

I talk with my wife and I try to get through it. I'm almost intentionally trying to hurt someone and that's not really part of my character. It's hard to let go of it, but I have to at some point because it's eating me up trying to hurt him. I'm trying to put pain on his heart, but it's killing me even more because I know how much it hurts him. He has a son that is a big football star and I've been a big player since I was in high school. I know he has pictures of me in his office and he tells everyone he has a son who plays football. They probably don't believe him and he has no proof. Again, I do it because I want him to feel what I went through. But it's wearing me out. It's poisoning me, but I don't know what to do. I picked up the phone one day to call him, but I just couldn't do it. Every day it's a struggle. Everything I went through up to this point, I want to forgive him. But it's so hard.

The first time I met him, I was at this restaurant and my mom called. It was like eleven or twelve at night. She called and said, "Baby, I've got someone I want you to meet." This is after my first year in college at Michigan State, the summer of 1998. So I wait there and she brings this guy in. I looked up and he was like six-four and he stuck his hand out and shook my hand. And when he shook my hand I automatically knew 'cause his hand was exactly like mine. Right then, my mom said, "This is your father," and I was so upset. I was so upset with my mom right then. She just didn't expect that and she just started crying.

I was thinking right then that she knew who my father was the whole time and she never told me. I was twenty the first time I saw him. I never knew who my real father was until that point. I always grew up thinking my father was someone else, like this boyfriend who used to come around and visit my mom. I thought this other guy was my father and then I found out who it is. She never told me and he never told me. He never said anything, he never explained. He lived like twenty minutes away, but I never knew. All those years and he never came by to tell me about himself.

So I guess that's why I'm this way now. I feel bad and I should call him, but I just want to walk into his office one day in the off-season and just sit there and say, "Why don't you tell me your story." I want to hear it from him. I think that will just give me an understanding. I can ask him, look him in the eye. Maybe that will let me be a little bit more at peace. It doesn't matter if it makes sense or not, I just need to hear it and maybe it will cure me of trying to purposely hurt him. It has been on my mind for months, but it's like real hard for some strange reason. I go through so much just thinking about it. Why?

Why am I putting myself through this right now? The way I see it, I don't have any parent right now. My mother raised me. She was the sole being, the reason why I'm here on this earth. I think I deserve some peace about it.

My father also showed up to my first college football game when we played against Colorado State. It was an exciting time for myself and my family. My mom was there and a bunch of other people. Here I was, the first person in my neighborhood ever to go to college—my whole neighborhood. It was a big day for myself, my family, and my hometown. I didn't know he was there until after the game. I was just so caught up in the game. It was on television, so I was excited.

I saw him and I ate dinner, talked, and had fun. I guess as the time went on I thought about all I went through and I was like, "The only times he comes around are when things are good." That's what happens with a lot of guys when they get to the pros. They don't know their fathers until they get to the NFL and then all of a sudden it's like, "Hey, I'm your dad." It has kind of made me distance myself from him.

Here I am, playing in my first game. Up to then, it was the greatest point of my life. I was living the dream, doing what I was doing since I was little, and basically he just showed up when everything was kind of on the better side of things. When I thought about it, it just didn't sit right with me.

I had contact with him when I was in Pittsburgh. We talked once in a while, but then I just kind of stopped. It was not a big thing where we had a fight or anything. I just didn't want to talk to him. Then he called my office line sometime in 2007. He got my number from somebody, I don't know how. But Tiffany was like, "Your father called you, baby." I was like, How the hell did he get my number?

Maybe he'll read this book and see how I feel. Maybe it will lead to us having a relationship, or an understanding. Maybe. We'll see.

8

Purple Haze

You want to know about Eli Manning? Here's a story that'll show you a side of him you never see. The day before the NFC Championship Game, we were getting ready to go to Green Bay, packing up and everything, doing all the stuff we gotta do. Some of the guys went out and got sandwiches for the rest of the guys, went over to Quiznos or whatever. Now, this was in the Giants Stadium locker room before we left.

So as the guys go over to get sandwiches, Eli took all the offensive linemen's shoes and painted them all purple. Actually, I don't know if he painted them or if he bought them. He might have actually bought them because they looked too good to be painted. I'm talking about hot purple, not like the dark purple. That shit was so funny. Those were some expensive shoes he got rid of from those guys, and when they got back and found these purple shoes, those guys were so mad. Hilarious.

That's Eli. He's a prankster. He's a good one, too. I don't know if that's how he deals with all the pressure of playing, but he's sharp when it comes to playing jokes. I think that's big for a lot of guys on our team. Having to play in the New York area, it's tense. But Eli and a bunch of the other guys keep it loose.

Probably Eli keeps it loose for himself. Those guys on the line are always getting him back. They'll hide his tie before road games. Richie Seubert and those guys love to play jokes on Eli.

The great part about the end of last season was that Eli was really on a roll. He was playing so great, he was so relaxed. I think everything just finally fell into place for him as far as knowing the offense, understanding what he had to do, and relaxing. He's just going to take off from there and keep going and going. But getting to that point has been really hard. He's not the kind of guy who walks around and keeps his head down all the time. He's got a few tricks up his sleeves.

Some of that pressure, you bring on yourself. I wanted to play in New York. I wanted to be on the big stage. You want that, you best understand that the fans are going to expect a lot. With Eli, it's the same thing, but even more. It's magnified because of that whole draft situation in 2004. He wouldn't go to San Diego. He wanted to be in New York instead. That's all on top of who he is, Peyton's brother, who his dad is, the whole thing.

From the first time I met Eli, we've been cool. It was at an off-season practice day in April after I signed there. In the locker room, they put our lockers side by side. So I met him and we had a good conversation. After a couple of minutes, Eli said, "You want to go catch a few?" So we went out and threw some routes. He said, "I'm glad to have you here." I said, "I'm happy to be here." When I first signed, I watched tape of him. I saw him play, I thought he had all the intangibles of a quarterback. That was one of the reasons I came to play with the Giants, to go play with a great quarterback, a great tight end, and a great running back. It was just kind of crazy to watch when I got here 'cause I think people wanted him to be like his brother right away. The funny thing is, Eli still won a championship at an earlier stage of his career and at a younger age than Peyton did. Playing in New York, though, people get on you if you're not playing as good as they expect. The players understand. It's like with me, my rookie year I wasn't that good. Eli only started seven games that first year before I got there. You have to give a person time to develop. Plus, it's quarterback, the hardest position in sports.

But New York, when the fans are on you . . . when it's like that, it's not a fun place to be. I looked at him and sometimes I could tell that he let stuff get to him. I remember after one game last year, either that Minnesota or Washington game when he had it really rough, I could see the tears of frustration kind of coming. It wasn't any of that boo-hoo stuff. He was just upset. He just shed a couple of tears because he was so upset and disappointed. People would say stuff about him, and if he didn't do as well as he wanted to, you could just look at his face and see it. You could hear it in his voice, too. He'd just say, "What's up, P?" but he wouldn't say it with the normal kind of tone. I would see him on Monday after he didn't do as well as he wanted to and you could just tell. For him, it's because he was the number one pick and the way that he came to New York with the whole trade thing. When he wouldn't play in San Diego, the fans were like, "Well, you wanted to be here, and now you can't even get your job done," so to speak. That was the outside perception. It's not that he came here and said a bunch of stuff. But the fans, they wanted him to be a star right then. That's not fair. In this game, everybody has to learn. You can't just walk out there, especially a quarterback, the hardest job on the field, the hardest position to play on the field.

Yeah. I say it's the hardest position on the field. Being a rookie, I can't even imagine how hard it would be. I got to play with him in his second year and I thought he was so advanced even then. But then I'd see some people out around town or something and they would say, "Man, what's wrong with Eli? How is he doing this, how is he doing that?" I would be, "Man, he's young, he's a great talent. You've got to give him time to get there. I didn't just get there overnight, I don't know anybody that has." You can understand that from a player's point of view. Come to training camp and just stand behind the quarterback in a team drill, and just look at how much madness is going on. I was like, Man, this is a rough position. But the fans wanted him to be Peyton overnight. After the Super Bowl, I remember saying I was just so happy for him because he'd got everybody off his back. I think that when he played well, he developed confidence and started believing more in himself. And then he almost got to playing with a swagger because he was so confident. I think that the way that he played with the stress of the last five or six games, in the Super Bowl . . . nobody's questioning anything about his toughness or whatever. He knows he can get the job done. Now he can just go out and be himself, and he don't have to worry about nothing else but concentrating on football, not trying to please anybody on the outside. Now he can just go play. I think that's the best feeling for a player.

Two games were real bad. Both of them were in 2005, my first season in New York—the Minnesota game and the Carolina playoff game. I think Minnesota was worse because he threw four picks and one of them went for a touchdown. But it was more because it was his first year starting and it was the first time the fans and the media really started to come down on him hard. I think it was even worse than when we played the Vikings this year and he had three returned for touchdowns. He kind of knew how to deal with it by this year. Back in 2005, it was his second year in the league and he threw four picks. It was so bad on TV and on radio and stuff after the game.

I picked up the phone and I called him and I said, "Hey, man, don't worry about it. We'll come back and get them next week." You could just tell how down he was. I was like, "Man, don't even worry about what anybody has to say. Just concentrate on what you got to do to go out there next week." He was like, "All right, P, thanks" and he just hung the phone up. I think that was one of the roughest times he had since I've been there. We were 6–2 and they came in and just hurt us. We thought we were going to beat the hell out of those guys. They didn't have anybody out there on that team. Then they beat the crap out of us. He took a lot of heat after that. I think that was the time when he started thinking about throwing interceptions. He didn't want to mess up. I think he was putting that pressure on himself not to mess up, and that would cause him not to play well sometimes. Starting with the Minnesota game, Eli threw twelve of his seventeen interceptions that year during the second half of the season.

But then we got to the Carolina game and, wow, that was bad. We didn't score a point. At home. I couldn't believe it. I thought, *I can't believe these guys are this much better than us.* Panthers coach John Fox had a great plan against us. They ran a lot of draws on our defense. Giants defensive end Osi Umenyiora had just become All-Pro, and he had fourteen and a half sacks that season and Mike Strahan was over on the other side doing his thing. Instead of letting Osi and Strahan be a factor in the running game or passing game, they ran a draw and let them come upfield. Draw, draw, draw, then pass and then a little screen, and that was their game plan. After running a draw the whole first and second quarters, the ends were not coming up the field as fast. Now Jake Delhomme had the defensive ends at his fingertips and he could just drop back, stay dropped back, and throw the pass. Now they would come up and look for draw. When they started to rush the passer again, you got them blocked easier because that big offensive lineman had time to set up.

For us on offense, Carolina defensive end Julius Peppers was over there dominating and we couldn't block him. I remember coming to the sidelines and I was like, *Damn, these mothers can't be that good. Julius Peppers can't be that good.* I looked at Jeremy and said, "Jeremy, he can't be that good." Jeremy looked at me and says, "Bro, he's good." I will never forget that. After Jeremy said that, I was thinking to myself, *He must be pretty damn good.* In the heat of the battle of the game, if Jeremy was saying, "Bro, he's good," Peppers must have been a hell of a player.

He was dismantling up front.

Peppers was the first guy I'd ever seen at that position who could come upfield, give a move to go outside, and who our right tackle, Kareem McKenzie, couldn't lay a hand on. I couldn't believe that. I was like, *Golly.* He would be rushing, going outside, and then he had this basketball crossover move, whew, and Kareem would be falling back and trying to get a hand on him. He did that two or three times. When a defensive lineman is so quick and the tackle is right in front of him and the tackle wasn't getting a hand on him, that guy's special. Peppers was creating so much pressure on Eli. They were running this defense that we called "four-middle." It would be like a quarters coverage with the four defensive backs, but then they would have this safety just run under and cut anything I was running on the inside, and he had two interceptions off those. That was the first time we had seen the defense called a four-middle. Somehow, they'd run that coverage and get the safety over there to cheat. It was like they were trying to funnel me to running a crossing route and then the other safety would come across and snatch a pick. They got two picks off that and we could never figure out how they were running it, what the timing of it was. I didn't even get a catch that day. I thought, *We can't score a point and I can't get a catch. How does that happen?* I think I only had three attempts come my way. Two of them were picks, and one of them got thrown on my head. Eli went ten of eighteen for 103 yards, got intercepted three times

and sacked four. We were on the sidelines the whole time saying, "Where is this guy coming from?" Carolina couldn't have
played it any better.

The next day after that game, I didn't go to the team meeting. I didn't think another team's defense could be so good that
I couldn't get the football. We didn't score a point; it was almost
embarrassing to get blown out at home, 23–0. I couldn't believe
we just got beat that bad. It was all over for the season, I was
upset and frustrated. I didn't think it really caused any trouble,
but a lot of people were upset that I didn't show up.

People both inside and outside the team were upset. I didn't
stick around long enough to really hear anything, either. I just
heard through the media that people were upset. I wasn't answering the phone, so I don't know whether it was coaches or
players or the owner. I was gone the next day. I ended up driving home to Virginia. Me and a couple of friends. That seems
like yesterday, but it was two years ago. We woke up the next
day and just drove to Virginia. I ended up staying in Virginia
for two or three days and then we jumped on the road and
drove all the way to Florida. I wasn't even trying to talk to anybody at that point. Football was not what I was really about at
that moment. After that game, Tiki had said all that stuff about
how we were outcoached and outplayed. But the fact is that it
almost looked that way. Either they are that good or they had a
hell of a plan against us. John Fox was the coach, and he coached
with those guys with the Giants before. He really had a good
understanding of our offense and defense. They had a hell of a
plan, man. I didn't say we were outcoached, but they had a hell
of a plan.

That off-season, Eli was talking about how he wanted me
and Jeremy to be up in New York, training together. I could
understand where he was coming from with the way that we
ended the year. I could sense some frustration. He wanted to

get extra work in, but my thing was the only reason I was in Florida, working my ass off, was I didn't want to be up in New Jersey training. The program that we had was not like we're going to be running outside in eighty-five, ninety degrees. Working out by running on turf, running in the bubble that we have, I don't really think that I'd be in good shape for fifty-degree weather. Both me and Shockey agreed on that, that's why he was down in Miami working there.

I'd been training in Florida for a couple of years. I was seeing my game start to get better and better. I just wanted to go to the place where I knew I'd be working hard, I'd be busting my ass. I didn't feel that Eli throwing the ball to just us two would make us better. I've been saying that forever. Just going out and throwing the ball, I can do that down here. I talked to Eli after he said it. He wanted to get right back to it. He was like, "Hey, you guys coming up?" I was like, "I'm down here training now." He said he would come down, but he never made it. I even invited him to come stay with me for a week if he wanted to come down here and throw and work out, but I didn't want to go back up there.

The next season, in 2006, stuff didn't change that much. To me, I could see that Eli was getting better. But we had so many things going on. Losing Amani Toomer early in the season really hurt. Amani was like Eli's security blanket. He knew Amani was always going to be there in certain situations. Eli got off to a really good start. That overtime game in Philadelphia was huge for him and his confidence. You got a real sense of how great he can be in a stressful situation. But after that Chicago game and then with Tennessee, we kind of fell apart and couldn't get any consistency. After the season, Coughlin put Kevin Gilbride in at offensive coordinator instead of John Hufnagel.

I think that Kevin being the quarterback coach with Eli in

2006 really helped. Kevin knew what we were trying to do on offense, and him having been an offensive coordinator, I think that all really helped. He knew all of Eli's strengths and how to make the offense work with them. The new offense him and Chris Palmer put in, it kind of simplified everything. I think Gilbride simplified it enough to the point where Eli could understand the offense from top to bottom, and once he understood the basic part of the offense, he could take it to the next level. That's kind of what we did. Gilbride put new terminology in. He ran enough stuff to where we weren't being predictable. Once we grabbed it, he took it to the next step on offense, putting in the check-with-me stuff where we have two plays called and Eli picks one after we get to the line. Once Eli got to that part, then he went through it all. We did the check-with-me stuff from the start of the season, but around the middle of the season, he had the full audible down. With the previous offensive coordinator, John Hufnagel, Eli could audible when we were in the two-minute offense, but it was all check-with-me stuff otherwise.

By the end of the season, it was sick, Eli had it down so good. You'd be in the huddle and you'd be like listening so close because the plays would be that long. Then sometimes we'd get to the line and he'd just check out of it all, pick the plays completely on the line. Sometimes Gilbride would be like, "What the fuck?" But a lot of the times it was, "Good job, good job." That's what he let Eli do, he let Eli become the field general. Eli knows the offense from top to bottom. He understands every defense they put out there. He's putting guys in the right positions. He's got the line going whatever way he wants it to go. Nobody ever said anything about his intelligence, because it's one of the best I've seen. But not everything is about checking out of plays. He's still working on the craft of being a quarterback.

This year, you could see in training camp that there was a difference. I said back then, "When the [receivers] are running into [defensive backs], he's actually stopping the guys from taking a hit. He's putting the ball in good places where it needs to be. He's trying to protect his receivers." He was being really accurate and really smart. Part of your job is to protect your receivers when you can. Obviously, you can't do it every time. There're times the receiver knows he's going to have to take a shot. But there're times when the quarterback can keep you from getting popped, too.

Once we got into the season, I thought he was playing pretty awesome, but he had those five or six games where he wasn't really too good. I think he was hurting, but he didn't say nothing. When he was able to throw the ball again, he was being real accurate with it. In the playoffs, he was just amazing. In fact, he really started playing great in that New England game at the end of the regular season. He had the one pick in the second half, but everything else against the Patriots was tight. We got to Tampa and they were running some odd defenses at him, waiting just a second and then trying to jump the routes with the linebacker. But he saw it all and didn't even come close to a mistake. Then, against Green Bay, he was just amazing. He was putting the ball in places in the Green Bay game where he was making my job just so easy. All I had to do was get open, catch, and run. There was a third-and-ten where I caught one on the sidelines and went out of bounds. It was on a rollout by Eli. Man, that may have been the best ball Eli threw all year. I had a similar one in the end zone against New England in the regular season when he rolled out that way and I went to the back of the end zone. The ball was out of bounds, but it was low enough that I could get to it and just keep my feet in. When he throws it like that and I catch it, it's a hell of a damn pass. When he does shit like that, I let him know. Man, that's exceptional. I couldn't believe he could do things like that. For some reason, when he gets into a run, when he's rolling out, he's just so accurate. When I see him doing stuff like that, I know his confidence goes to a different level. He can do just about anything his mind wants him to do with confidence like that. He just gets so confident that he walks around, plays with a swagger, and he knows he is going to do good.

And like I said, he was playing his jokes. Yeah, he got me once, too. Me, I was on the job, out there catching balls with the JUGS machine that fires footballs at you. So I was like one of the last guys to come in. I came in and we've got our towels on our stools for when we take a shower and stuff. I took my sweaty pads and shit off and I wiped my face down with my towel and everybody was laughing. I said, "What the hell, man, what's so funny?" So they told me that Eli just sat on my towel with his bare ass coming out of the shower. He was soaking wet, sat on my towel, and kind of did this little shake with his ass. Then I showed up and wiped my face on the towel and everybody busted out. I was so mad, but I can't be mad because he's the quarterback, what am I going to do to him? So he came back and I looked at him and he was like, "What?" I'm like, "Man, why you do me like that? I don't mess with you, why do you mess with me?"

He was like, "What did I do? What did I do?"

I said, "You sat on my towel with your bare ass."

"Oh, I did? I thought it was mine. My bad, P Money."

"All right, man, whatever." I got him back once. I put some grapes in his shoes, so when he put his foot in his little loafers, he made jelly.

9

It's a Job, but It Can Be Fun

The first time I sat down with Tom Coughlin, I immediately got the vibe that he wasn't comfortable with me. He said, "I know you have heard all these things about me." I said, "Why would I hear things about you? I know I hear you are a hard-ass." He said, "Yes, I am demanding, but don't listen to what is going on. I know you have some guys who are former players around you who will talk to you, but I just want to win. There are going to be some changes, the rules, things that are just different. Don't let that affect why you are here."

Now, when he said *demanding* and *rules*, I didn't think it was going to come down to everything I did, every move I made. That was my first year on the team and I was thinking, *How bad can this guy be?* If you started your career with the Giants, you're okay. You just know this is the way it's going to be. The discipline and all the things we do differently, you just think it's part of the deal. You would think that is the way it's got to be. But I came from the laid-back environment in Pittsburgh. Work was fun. Going to work there, we laughed and we joked. We paid attention. When we stepped on the practice field, we worked our asses off and then we went home. I knew like the first minute I practiced with Coughlin that it was different.

So I'm there for an April off-season practice day and I'm getting ready to go out there. I get my jersey ready. I cut off the bottom of it and then I cut off the part that goes around the neck 'cause that's kind of tight. Then I put my white T-shirt that I always wear to practice on underneath. The guys look at me and say, "Are you trippin'?" I'm like, "What? What'd you mean?" They just said, "Watch." So we get out there and Coughlin sees my jersey and he says right away, "We don't alter our equipment." I'm like, Are you serious? Then he said about my T-shirt: "We only wear Giant-issued clothing. I know you come from a place where they let you do what you wanted to do, but that is not here." I was like, *Holy shit, this is serious.* This is practice. Wow. So we come out for the next practice and I had a brand-new jersey on.

But when I played my first couple years here, it was just so work-oriented. It made going to work not really fun. You got up and went, "Oh, man, I gotta go to work tomorrow, damn." Everywhere you had to be you had to be five minutes early or that was considered late. You couldn't be out of uniform. You had to lift with this type of shirt on. You couldn't drink alcohol on the team plane.

Now, Tom had a good reason for it. You can't say it didn't work because we won the championship. But from a player perspective, we looked at it and it looked like there was no reason for it except it's the way that Tom is. He wants to make us the way he is. That's just how he likes things run. If you like your bed made a certain way or your shoes laced a certain way, you have to change it to the way he wants. If you go on the road, you are going to do it that way, his way. He's trying to change us to do it his way.

Ernie Accorsi talked about Tom and me in the book *The GM.*

He said, "Tom has had trouble with him. Tom keeps trying to change him. I said, 'Tom, Holy Cross was not one of the schools Plax was considering when he went to Michigan State, okay? If you don't want to coach these kinds of kids, then go to Holy Cross.'" That was funny and it was true.

It was all the picky stuff. You have to weigh in before practice and after practice to check your weight loss. If you don't, it's a fifty-dollar fine. Some guys can lose a lot of weight in a hurry. I can lose six or seven pounds in a practice. If that happens, I'm on alert for dehydration. You can't let that go on. You have to get water back in your system or you get dehydrated. But the thing is that, by now, if you're a veteran guy, you know that. You know you can't drop a bunch of weight and feel good. I get the point about weighing in, but what's the point of the fine? That's not going to make me do it more than I already want to. Look, I'm 227 pounds all day long, all week long. My weight just doesn't change. I'm not like the big offensive and defensive linemen who can gain a bunch of weight in a hurry. That's just not how I was built. Guys like me who weigh in the same since they've been there, sometimes you just don't see the point about weighing in. But it's how he likes it.

Tom and me are just different. He is a special individual. He is a little off the chart. He is a real neat freak. You go in his office to talk to him, and before you sit down, he has to make sure everything is in line, that the papers are all straight, even if they're already in a stack. He is one of those guys—just a different guy. He kind of lives by the old creed, like General Custer, Vince Lombardi, and Jack Youngblood. He is that era. He lives through great quotes. He'll even tell you, "That's the way I live." Every day he has a new quote for you. He must be a hell of a book reader. There's no way he could come up with those every day unless he does a lot of reading. He does come up with a lot of good ones.

We had a big falling-out in 2006. First, I didn't feel good one day and I had done a lot of lifting already. So I went and told the strength coach that I was going to skip my lifting that day. The coach went and told Tom, and I got fined. I think it was like $1,800. There's all sorts of stuff you get fined for. Where do you want me to start? Not wearing a tie on the plane coming back from a game on the road. I was the late king. I was late so much, it was $1,500 here, $1,500 there, just for being late.

And this is where we really got in trouble in 2006. It was two weeks into training camp and my wife was pregnant. It was our first baby and there were only certain days she can go and get the ultrasound. This is the ultrasound where we're going to find out the sex of the baby. So I was excited and I came in like two weeks before that and said, "Coach, I'm going to be late this day." It was a Tuesday and normally we had Tuesdays off. Again, I was telling him about this like two or three weeks in advance. But then I realized that we had to play a Sunday-night game that week in New York. So we were going to have Monday off and be back early Tuesday. So I went back and I said, "Coach, you know I'm not going to be here Tuesday morning, I got that ultrasound, right?" Tom says, "I know." So I got to work about eleven o'clock that morning. I missed the morning meeting or whatever, but I got there as soon as I could. I was so happy because I found out it was a boy. I was telling all the guys. It was great.

Then I got to my stool and there is a fine sheet in my locker and I was like, what's the fine for? I open it up and it's a $2,000 fine. So I took the fine sheet and I went to Tom and I said, "Coach, I got a fine sheet." He said, "Yeah, I know, you missed your meeting this morning." I said, "But I told you in advance." He said, "Yeah, but you were just telling us you weren't going to be there. But you missed a meeting and that's a fine." I was like,

I broke the Michigan State record for receptions and yards in a game on this catch against Michigan in 1999. *(Michigan State University Sports Information)*

I could really cut at Michigan State. *(Michigan State University Sports Information)*

One of my thirteen catches in my final college game as we beat Florida 37–34.
(Andy Lyons/Getty Images)

Catching a touchdown for Pittsburgh against New England on October 31, 2004.
I ran the same pass pattern when I caught the game-winning touchdown in the
Super Bowl. *(Andy Lyons/Getty Images)*

Rapping with Bill Cowher,
the coolest coach I ever had.
*(George Gojkovich/Contributor,
Getty Images)*

Celebrating a TD run by Jerome Bettis in the AFC Championship Game in 2005.
"The Bus" won the Super Bowl the next year and retired a winner.
(Paul Spinelli/Contributor, Getty Images)

Jeremy Shockey and I became tight after working out together in Miami once I joined the Giants. *(Chris McGrath/Getty Images)*

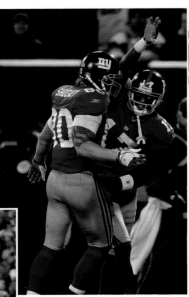

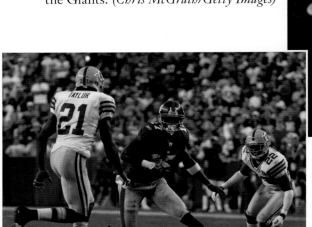

I scored a touchdown against Washington on September 23, 2007, running past Carlos Rogers and Sean Taylor for 33 yards. It was the last time I played against Taylor—he was killed a few weeks later in a shooting at his home in Miami. I went to Taylor's funeral. *(Diamond Images/Contributor, Getty Images)*

Before we played the Bucs in the playoffs on January 6, 2008, Ronde Barber got me with some comments I took as insults to my ability. *(Matthew Stockman/ Getty Images)*

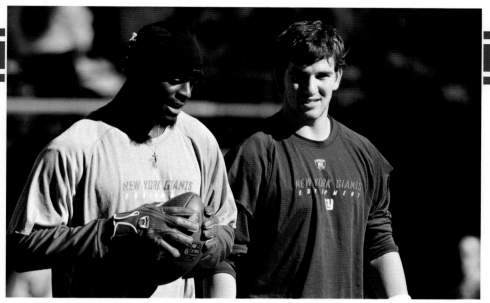

My man Eli and I before the Dallas playoff game on January 13, 2008.
Eli didn't throw an interception for three straight playoff games.
(Wesley Hitt/Contributor, Getty Images)

I was so cold before the Green Bay game on January 20, 2008, that I only
warmed up for about ten minutes before the game. It was crazy.
(Evan Pinkus/Contributor, Getty Images)

One of my eleven catches against Pro Bowl cornerback Al Harris. Our 23–20 win in overtime against Green Bay in the NFC Championship Game put us in the Super Bowl. *(Tom Hauck/Contributor, Getty Images)*

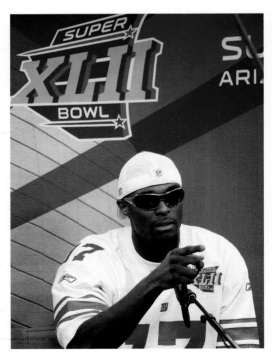

Answering questions during Media Day on the Tuesday before the Super Bowl. My prediction of a victory for the Giants made some headlines. What was I supposed to say, that I thought we'd lose? *(Paul Spinelli/Contributor, Getty Images)*

Warming up before the Super Bowl against New England. My knee was killing me so much that I almost didn't play. *(Ben Liebenberg/Contributor, Getty Images)*

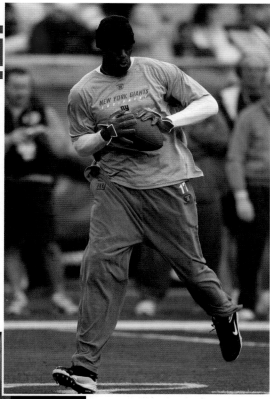

Giving thanks after catching the game-winning touchdown in our 17–14 victory over the previously undefeated Patriots in Super Bowl XLII on February 3, 2008. *(Paul Spinelli/Contributor, Getty Images)*

Tiffany and I celebrate the Super Bowl victory at a postgame party. *(Bennett Raglin/Contributor, Getty Images)*

My boy, Elijah, means the world to me. I was so happy to have him and Tiffany there to experience winning the Super Bowl, even if he is a little young to know what's going on. *(Heinz Kluetmeier/Contributor, Sports Illustrated)*

Are you shitting me? If that's the way it's going to be, then what was the purpose of me telling you? I'd be better off if I didn't tell you anything. So that was when me and him ran into a real problem that year. He was so big on saying, "You can come to my office, you can tell me anything. I want us to have a better relationship." But after that, that crossed the line. We just weren't going to see eye to eye. I paid the fine, though.

Meanwhile, I was thinking, Man, you can't win with this guy. You know what, I'm just going to come to work and play ball and go home. From a personal standpoint, it was just hard. I mean, we get paid great and we're playing a game and all that. Yeah, it's not like a real job. But there are things about it that can still suck if you make it that way. It really ought to be fun. You've got to work hard, but you can enjoy it and appreciate it. You get to do stuff that other people dream about, so that's great.

Tom and me don't have the best relationship, but it's not about him. It's about me fulfilling my accountability to my teammates. I overlook all the rules and all those things because I have a job to do. If I go out and mess up and don't do what I'm supposed to do, then the other guys suffer. I'm not an excuse guy. I can't say I don't like the coach, so I'm not going to do such and such or I'm not accountable for what happens. My job is to be accountable to my teammates. So I overlook all those things that bug me, the rules. At the end of the day it is really all about how I've performed.

Not everyone is like that. There are a lot of guys who will say, "Oh, it's the coach's fault that I didn't play well." You've got to have guys who can look themselves in the mirror and the camera and be honest and say, "Man, I screwed up." But when the team isn't doing well, that's hard. Everyone wants to put up a protective shell around themselves.

How do I help the new guys, the rookies and guys from

other teams, deal with it? I don't. They got to deal with it. I got to deal with it. I say to them, there is no way that I can help you get around a situation that I can't even help myself to get around. A guy like myself who walks up to Tom and says they've got a problem with something, that's the best you can do to deal with him. You see where I'm coming from? Guys say, "Hey, how can I do this? How do I handle this rule? I don't want to go talk to him." I say, "Man, I don't have an answer for you. I wish I could help you, but I can't. You just got to deal with it."

The thing is that Tom wants to treat everybody the same, whether you've been in the league for ten or eleven years, if you've got a wife and kids, or if you're a rookie. It's the same for everyone. But it really shouldn't be that way. If you've been around and proved yourself, you don't want to have to go through what the rookies are going through. You want to be catered to. Take a practice off, let your body get better. You want to be sort of catered to, but he wants everyone treated the same.

I thought he just wanted to win, but here he was with all these rules and he was not doing as well as he wanted to. We were really good, but we were not winning. Everyone got frustrated in 2006. We were in full pads for sixteen weeks. The whole season, we were in full pads every Wednesday. We weren't hitting the whole time, but just wearing the pads that long sucked. We didn't want to be doing that after we went through a whole off-season and training camp and now we were in the season. We especially didn't want to do it when we were losing. That's the thing, guys will put up with a lot of stuff when you're winning. In 2005, we went 11–5 and thought we were going great until we get to Carolina in the playoffs. That was a shock, but it was like we just ran into a game where everything went bad. The next year, we started fast and then couldn't finish, couldn't get anything going, and then everybody was on edge.

At the end of 2006 it was pretty crazy. Tiki was talking to the press about this and that. The press was making a big deal out of his retirement all season. Jeremy was talking to the press about Coughlin. But the only thing I was really saying is, "Hey, this can be fun. It should be fun. We should be enjoying it." I don't know if management noticed what I was saying. They didn't come talk to me about it. But that's what they obviously talked to the coach about.

Everybody was wondering if Tom was going to come back, but I wasn't really too concerned. If he came back, he came back. If not, somebody else was going to coach us. Again, my thing is that it's not about the coach or his rules or anything like that. I have to be accountable in this job to my teammates.

Coming back in 2007, Tom was a little lighter. He showed his human side. I think he realized that yes, this is a business, but you got to appreciate this job and say, hey, this can be fun. I think he realized from a coaching standpoint, he was just so grateful to come back for one year to prove himself. I think he felt he had to make some changes. Sometimes a coach or a player has to make changes to better himself and sometimes he's got to make changes to better somebody else. It doesn't matter how old or young you are. A lot of us make changes to get better.

When you're the head coach, and you see that things you're doing aren't working, I would think from a personal standpoint you would have to make some changes. When Tom lightened up, everybody noticed. I could walk up to him and have a good conversation with him. He was like the total opposite of what he had been before. I just noticed that he was being a little bit more outgoing with guys. He looked at me one day and said, "How's your family, Plax?" and I'm thinking, Is this the same Tom Coughlin? It was good.

The other thing is that he got a sense of humor about himself. We're always in the locker room cracking on guys not being athletic. It's the middle of the season and Tom Coughlin was walking through the locker room and he tripped over this snag in the carpet. And he didn't look like an athlete at all. He hit the ground and the guys were snickering. They couldn't really laugh 'cause they wanted to see if he was all right first. But his glasses went flying and his Giants cap went way over here. It was hysterical.

And he popped up and he said, "Did you guys see that? I looked like a real athlete there, huh?" He smiled and made fun of himself. After practice, Richie Seubert lay on the floor and we put the athletic tape around him so it looks like one of them outlines from a murder scene. Then we got a pair of glasses and a hat and put them around the tape. It was perfect. So we're all sitting in the locker room and guys are looking out for the coach. Somebody whispers, "He's coming, he's coming." He walks in, looks down, and says, "Who did this?" Everyone busted out laughing. He laughed and shook his head. It was funny. Two years ago, he would have been mad. He probably would have tried to find out who it was and fined him.

During the Super Bowl week, the old coach Jim Mora Sr. was talking to Michael Strahan. He asked Strahan if Coughlin had really changed. Michael said, "Well, he's smiling. And he uses the word *fun*. I never expected that out of him . . . After practice, if it's not the greatest practice, he doesn't come and jump down your throat. He'll say this is not the caliber we expect." Stuff like that was a good change for Tom. Just lightened it up.

He had to do that. The whole organization was on him to lighten up. The owners wanted to see him succeed because they hired him in the first place and he *is* a good coach. He knows what he's doing. But it had to change. I think that's fair. Tom still had stuff that was important to him. Like on the first day of training camp, he talked about how he wanted us to just shut up and play. So I said, "He wants it to be a quieter year; we want a lot of things. But I guess we'll try to abide by keeping it quiet. That's just not the character of some of the guys that we have on this team. But I guess we'll try . . . A little bit of trash talking doesn't hurt anybody. It adds a little extra incentive to the game for me. We'll see what happens."

Or it was like when I supposedly made my big prediction. We were at media day and people were asking me about it and I didn't back down. I said, "I am going to say it again, the goal is to win the football game. It is not to come here and just play. The goal is to come here and win. That's why we are here." I said, "We will win the football game." What do you want me to say? The media starts asking Tom about it and he said, "That's not the way we have done things all season." He said a little something to me about it, but he didn't jump down my throat about it and want to fine me. Hey, that was a change.

10

Living Through 2006

I guess when you start to talk about the 2007 season, you gotta start back in 2006 because it was so weird. I mean, it was real weird. Not just how the season went, but all the stories around it. We had the whole Tiki Barber thing going on with the media, like it was some big deal to us. The fact is that nobody even cared about it. Seriously, they made it out to be this big deal, but we didn't really feel it on the inside. I don't care, nobody cares if a guy is going to retire. As long as you're playing hard and if you go out and you win, nobody cares. Just come play hard on Sunday, win, go home, and everybody is happy. It's business, that is how it is. I've had games where I've had a hundred, a hundred forty yards and we lose. It doesn't matter how I played. It doesn't mean anything. It does personally, but it feels so much better if you win. I tell everyone that all the time. My job as a ballplayer is to work hard, be a good teammate, and play hard on Sunday. That's my job. That's what I do. That's what Tiki did. He still played hard, so I didn't have a problem. I didn't have a problem with him doing all that broadcasting stuff.

What I had a problem with was, knowing him and being a teammate, I was expecting that when he went into broadcasting, he would be better to us. You would think he would be one of our biggest supporters. But he was sort of a chameleon, not even a fan. But that's cool. After the Super Bowl, he came into our locker room and we still loved him. But it was like the stuff at the beginning of the 2007 season between him and Eli. Tiki ripped Eli, saying Eli wasn't a leader and that Eli's attempts to be a leader were "comical." What I said when that came out was, "It's not fair to Eli. I hate to see those two guys go at it like that. They shared the same team jersey for a number of years and shouldn't go at each other through the media. If they have a problem, they should pick up the phone and talk to each other." They've known each other for years. It just shouldn't happen. They're good friends and they should talk like that.

But as far as Tiki saying he was retiring early in the season, it didn't mean anything to us. We were just trying to get into the playoffs. There was no drop-off in his play when he said he was retiring. The guy was one of the top two or three backs in the league. He wasn't taking plays off. If anything, he was probably running harder. He was probably playing harder. He was going out there and giving everything that he had, and we never had problems with him. It was just the people on the outside making an issue of it. He was still our leader.

Now, Tiki and Coughlin had a problem. That went all the way back to after the playoff game against Carolina after the 2005 season. We got shut out at home, 23–0. I mean, that was embarrassing. So after the game, Tiki talked about how we got outcoached. Other guys are picking up on that, like Jeremy Shockey. So the media was going crazy with that. Tiki was saying stuff that he thought had to be said and that's fine, but only certain guys can say stuff like that. Tiki had been there for ten years and he had built up credibility with the fans. He had been there and he could say that without worrying about getting run out of town. For me, I think very carefully about what I'm going to say, 'cause I can't do that the same way as somebody like Tiki. There are things that people will say that I can't say because the fans will take it totally out of perspective and they'll be like, "Burress, you can get the hell out of here."

And it wasn't even all about Tiki. It was just that he was part of the news all season, it seemed. It started off with that big game against Indianapolis, the Manning Bowl. Here it is the opening game, in our stadium, and we walk in and we see Peyton Manning on the front of our game-day program with Eli. I think that's the first time in history that an opposing player is on the front cover of our game program. There was Peyton Manning and Eli on the front. I was like, damn, he's so good, he made *our* cover. That's the first time I've ever seen that. We still talk about it to this day. It was really unbelievable. That game was a fun game to play in, it was really intense. First game of the season, Sunday night, and the most-watched NBC event. It was really crazy and they ended up with the championship. Them guys beat us by five points and then when they won it, it was like, damn, that was another game we should have won that season.

Philadelphia was the next game and we came back from being down by seventeen in the fourth quarter to win in overtime. That was a great game for Eli. We were in the two-minute offense practically the whole fourth quarter, calling all the plays. Amani Toomer went off for twelve catches, 137 yards, and two touchdowns. I went over 100 yards and caught the game winner in overtime. Just an amazing game. The next week, we went out to Seattle and got way behind. It was 42–3 after three quarters, but then we went wild in the fourth quarter again and almost pulled it out. After the game, Jeremy Shockey said we got "outplayed and outcoached." He finished by telling the reporters to "write that down." It's pretty much the same thing Jeremy said after the Carolina playoff game in January, so it wasn't that big a thing to me. But it made headlines again and Coughlin was all sour. Jeremy then kind of backed away from it the next day. I don't know if they talked, but Coughlin doesn't like finger-pointing.

Then we got on a roll, won five straight. Suddenly a bunch of people thought we had the best team in the NFC. We went to Dallas and kicked their ass so bad they had to change quarterbacks. The hype was starting to get going and we were getting ready to play the Bears at home.

We were playing pretty good in the first half. We missed some chances in the game, but we were leading at halftime and then we were only down by four in the fourth quarter when Coughlin called for this fifty-two-yard field goal into the wind on a rainy night. Jay Feely was kicking, but it was brutal conditions and the Bears had Devin Hester back there. The offense came to the sideline and I was watching the field goal. It was short. When I saw Hester catch that ball, all I did was look on the field because I just knew he was going to return it. Just looking at all the big bodies running around out there, they didn't stand a chance. It was all offensive linemen who were blocking for the field goal. I saw Hester catch it, and I was like, *It don't look good.* They got caught off guard. That field goal was so long, some of the guys were actually jogging down and some of the guys were standing there looking. Hester took two or three slow steps. He was just walking. Then he just stepped on the gas. He returned that thing 108 yards. That play right there, that put a bullet in our back for the season. We never recovered from that. That's one of our least-favorite plays ever. We didn't win two games in a row for the rest of the year. They ended up killing us 38–20 with Rex Grossman just going off. Rex Grossman was killing us. Wow. We lost to the Bears. Then we went to Jacksonville and they just pounded us. The game was close in the third quarter. I scored a touchdown to make it 13–10. But then they just never stopped running on us. They finished with forty-three carries for 165 yards and we just couldn't get them off the field and then we couldn't move the ball enough when we had it.

But then came the Tennessee game. This is when Vince Young had his big coming-out party. We made Vince Young look great. We were up 21–0 after three quarters and then they came back and beat us 24–21. That's the game where Mathias Kiwanuka had Young in his grasp on fourth-and-seven and let Vince go because he thought the play is dead. Coughlin just flipped out on us. He went ape shit. Man, he went crazy. His face was probably as red as it was during the Green Bay game in the NFC Championship when it was freezing cold. He was hot at the end of the Tennessee game. Right on the sidelines, he went off. He was yelling and cursing. He was pissed off. We were all pissed. Not just that we lost, but more the way we lost. It had been 21–0 and then we let them back in. We just needed a stop or something, but that's when the Vince Young show started. The thing about him was, when he was running he don't look all that fast. It don't even look like he's running, but nobody could catch him. He's quick, man. For some reason, I get the feeling he's more dangerous than Mike Vick.

The other play that got all the attention was one with me, and this one just took off in the media being that we lost. It was the fourth quarter and we were at our own thirty-five-yard line. It was second-and-four and we took a shot over the top. I was being covered by Pacman Jones, who's like five-nine or something. You figure it's a pretty safe chance to take. But Eli overthrew it. Now, usually I make the catch on those circus plays and I didn't make an excuse on that one. In fact, I made the catch on exactly that same play against Ronde Barber and Tampa Bay in another game.

Basically, if someone is in front of me, what I usually do is run to him, jump over him, and use my wingspan and my height. Even if I can't get it, I usually can break it up, make sure the defender can't get it if he has me beat to the point. I usually cut behind the defender to do that on the jump ball. I just cut between the defender's path and the path of the ball. That's what I was trying to do. But before I could get off the ground, I ran into Pacman and now I couldn't jump. I lost my footing and I couldn't get off the ground. Instead of me cutting behind him to get the ball, I kind of pushed him into the play. I helped him get to the ball and then he grabbed it. I was flat-footed and I couldn't react to him. Pacman returned that interception to set them up for their first touchdown as they came back. Then Pacman got another interception later in the game and returned a punt. He went off and so did Vince.

But the other thing about that play is that by me running into him, it also made me look like I had stopped. It made me look like I quit the play. After the game, I couldn't break that down for anyone, I couldn't say what happened. Again, I wasn't into making excuses. Here we were with three straight losses after we were 6–2 just three weeks ago. That Tuesday, Mike Strahan went on WFAN radio in New York like he did every week and talked about the play. I didn't know it at the time. He said: "It's a shame, because Plaxico is a great player and a good guy to be around, but at the same time you're judged by your actions on the field and you can't give up, you can't quit, because you're not quitting on yourself, you're quitting on us. We work too hard all together to have that type of stuff happen, and Plaxico is one of the guys who works hard. I don't quite understand what his motivation is, or what his lack of motivation is in those type of situations. I'm pretty sure I'm going to try to see what it is and try to see if I can talk to him about it. He's too great of a player to have people look at him and think he's a quitter. Don't be labeled as a guy who's a sometimes player, I-play-when-I-want-to type of attitude. He's too good for that."

It didn't mean anything to me. Hey, I would have appreciated it if he had walked over to me and said something to me, but I got nothing bad to say about him. Just come up to me and say it, man-to-man. But now everyone knew how he felt, except me. I didn't know about it until I got to work the next day and the media hit me with the questions. I was like, what is going on with this? Then I actually read the radio transcript and I was like, wow. Really, I didn't know about it at all till I got there that day. Still, Stray is my friend. After the reporters left, I walked over to him and said, "Hey, if that's how you felt, you could have walked ten paces to your right and told me." I didn't hold a grudge. Like I said, Stray is my guy. He said, "That's not the way I wanted it to come out." It was over right there. I forgave him.

When he came back this year after missing training camp, I was right there welcoming him back, happy to see him. Turns out, he didn't know exactly what happened on the play, either. But there was so much going on with the team. We were losing and he said I quit on a play. I didn't really appreciate that he said I quit, but then the whole thing blew up. The reporters were asking me, then everybody was in front of his locker and it was just a zoo. He got into it with that reporter from ESPN and this stuff is so beside the point. We're just trying to win a football game somehow.

That whole situation is just an example of what I mean when you hear how guys can lose it so fast in this game. When you play pro football, it's like two or three plays can determine the whole season, can affect your whole frame of mind. How you handle that will tell you everything about yourself. If you are going to have any doubt, you're not going to survive in this business. Just ask yourself, how can players be so great one week and be down the next? It's all about your mind-set. Look, some days I'm tired. I'm playing, but I just want to go home. But fatigue is physical and you fight through that. But if your mind is true all the time, you can focus on the job. That's why I don't let things affect me in how I'm playing my game. I don't read the newspapers. I really don't. That's why I didn't know what Stray had to say until the reporters asked me about it and showed it to me. I had gone through that kind of stuff in Pittsburgh where I worried about what was written. I was young. I listened to whatever anybody had to say and I got caught up in trying to defend myself verbally instead of letting my performance on the field do the talking. The best way to defend myself as a player is to just go show you. I could talk and say anything I want to in front of the microphone, but that doesn't matter. The best way to defend Plaxico Burress is to go show you.

The next week we played Dallas at home. Earlier in the season, we had beaten them. But Tony Romo had come in and now he was on a hot streak. We knew it was going to be a tough game and that's exactly how it played out. Nobody was ever up by more than a touchdown. We were just going back and forth. I caught a touchdown with about a minute left to tie it up at twenty. It was a fade pass over Anthony Henry. But right after Dallas got the ball back, Romo hit a forty-two-yard pass to Jason Witten to put them in field-goal range. They hit the field goal with one second left and now we've lost four in a row. We were back to .500 at 6–6. Over the last four weeks, we went back and forth. We beat Carolina and Washington—Tiki played great in the Washington game, the last game of the season. We also lost pretty bad to Philadelphia and New Orleans.

The thing is that it was like there were three plays that just totally wrecked our season. There was the Bears game, Tennessee, and then Dallas. It was like one or two plays that caused us to get whipped. Instead of being 11–5 the way we were in 2005, we were 8–8 and struggling. We still got into the playoffs, though, and we went down to Philly to play the Eagles, who beat us a couple of weeks before at home. We actually had a lead in that game with seven minutes to go, but then they scored on a pass by Jeff Garcia and put us away with an interception return on the next play after we got the ball back. That was brutal for Eli the way that happened. But the funny thing was that we started playing pretty good on the road, which carried over into 2007. Both the games we won in December were on the road and the other home game was when we got beat pretty bad by New Orleans. Anyway, we were in Philly again and it was close all game.

It's the fourth quarter and we came back from being down 20–10 to tie it at 20 with 5:04 left. The frustrating part is we could have been up by two touchdowns. Eli missed me on this one pattern in the back of the end zone. A winning team can't miss plays like that. That's the big difference with him. He's not missing those now. He has learned and made progress. But at the time, we were playing a team that was not as good as we are and we gave them a chance to stay in the game. It was a great call on the play. It was a double hook and I had double coverage, but Tiki was supposed to run up to the goal line. As soon as he did that, the double came off me and I'm wide open in the back of the end zone. I threw my hands up in frustration because, like I said, you can't miss those. It was just one of those plays that happen. I never asked Eli about it. I didn't have to, he understood. He's a smart guy. He learned when he watched that.

We didn't get the lead and then they march down at the end and kicked a forty-yard field goal with no time left. I was just like, Man, well, see if I can do it again and see if I can get me a championship in year eight. I just thought, I have to start all over again from scratch next year. Now, the previous year when Carolina beat us, I didn't go to the meeting and it created a big stir. This year, I went. It was different. We played our hearts out against Philly. I'm pretty sure there are things we could have done differently, but we left it all out there for that game. It wasn't like the Carolina game. It was just frustrating. I just wanted to go in and get it over with at the meeting.

Everybody in the media was asking about whether Coughlin was going to be back. Guys on the team were wondering. Really, it didn't matter to me whether he came back or not. My job isn't to worry about who is going to be the coach or offensive coordinator. My job is to worry about Plaxico Burress, and get myself ready to play. Beyond that, my wife was ready to give birth, so I had bigger things on my mind. After the baby was born and we got settled, I was out of there. I spent my whole off-season down in South Florida. I ended up having surgery on my left ankle by Dr. Robert Anderson in Charlotte to take the bone spurs out and I started rehab right away. It was funny, I was riding around in my motorized scooter for a long time. Byron Leftwich came down to Florida to train and he saw me and said, "What the hell are you doing?" I told him I was riding around on my scooter, like them old people you see. Dr. Anderson even said, "I always tell guys if you don't need surgery, don't get it." I had just scored ten touchdowns that season, so I played through it, but I could feel it was getting worse. I decided to get it done.

When I got it done, I was regretting it a little because I was still hurting in training camp.

My Man Shock

I've talked about tight end Jeremy Shockey a few times in this book. Shock is my boy, we're great friends. We have the same agent and after I signed with the Giants, I got his number from Drew Rosenhaus and called him. I told him he was one of the reasons I signed with New York. I wanted to play with a tight end who had the ability to get down the seam of the field and open up the back side for the X receiver, which is where I play. He's a Miami guy and I told him I was going to be working out down there and then he told me he'd join me. I'd been expecting he might show up once or twice, but we ended up working out like four days a week, busting ass trying to get better.

He's like my brother, man, and unfortunately, he couldn't play in the Super Bowl after he broke his leg in the game against Washington in December. Obviously, Shock went through a lot after this, watching us win the Super Bowl. After he broke his leg in the season, I just felt so bad for him. He plays so hard and gives his all in every game, but he can't seem to catch a break. When you lose a guy like that, it's so hard to replace his production and he's kind of like an emotional leader.

He was at the game and was on the sidelines with us in the

second half, cheering us on, and I'm telling you, he's going to be more motivated than ever to show people how good he is. He's going to come back stronger. I'm telling you, I see it already.

But it's not like people make out that we're a better team without Shock. That's just not the case. What happened after Shock got hurt is that people like Kevin Boss stepped up and Eli really took off. I think Eli realized that without Shock out there, he needed to step it up even more and be that much better.

The people who said Shock was upset with our success, how would they know? How would they know if he was upset when he was in Texas with his mom? All that stuff is just wrong. Was the media sitting on the couch beside him? He's one of the fiercest competitors I've ever been around. I talked to him all the time when he was at home. I would say, "What you doing, man?" And he'd say, "I'm just chilling with my mom." "All right, well, tell Mom I said what's up?" He's just a different fellow and a lot of people don't understand where he comes from when he talks. He speaks from his heart all the time.

It's like what my mom used to say about thinking with your head instead of your heart. It's hard for him to do that. I tell him all the time, "Hey, man, you just can't talk to people like that." He's like, "I can talk the way I want to talk to them." I'm like, "See, that's what I'm saying?" He calms down a little and says, "All right, bro, I understand, I understand." I'm like, "Man, look, just go tell them you're sorry." Then he gets going again. "I ain't telling them I'm sorry." That's just how he is, but he's a good dude at heart.

People always ask me, "Why do you and Shock have this great relationship?" It's because he is just one of those people who, when you talk to him, you ain't got to worry about getting a knife in your back. That's just the type of person he is. If he's got a problem with you, he's just going to tell you how he feels. He don't care if you don't like him or if anybody else likes him. He's going to always defend me, regardless, and I'm always going to defend him, regardless. If he was wrong, I'll go tell him he was wrong to his face, man-to-man. I don't go to the media or anybody else and say he shouldn't have said that. I go to him. If I got a problem with something that he says, I go tell him. I say, "You shouldn't have said that, you should have said it this way, then there wouldn't have been a problem."

Some of the coaches are always saying to me, "Hey, go talk to your boy. Make sure everything's all right." Some games he'll have one catch or no catches at halftime, and you come back and he's getting five straight balls, then he's ready to go. It's not that he's pouting or anything, he wants to feel like he's a part of what's going on. He's a competitor. I understand it. I'm like that, too, and I like it when the coaches are coming to me and asking me about what I see or what we can do. But that's regular talking. With Shock, he's kicking over Gatorade jugs, helmets, everything. That's just who he is. He's that much of a competitor and everybody sees that and says, "Oh, he has a temper, he's having a tantrum." No, he wants the ball. He wants to go in and try to help us win and make us better. If we get him the ball more, then we wouldn't be in this nail-biting situation. He wants to help get us out so we can win football games easily. People just construe it the wrong way.

It's like in practice. Man, I've got to tell him to chill out sometimes. I'm like, "Yo, you don't have to run sixty yards when you catch the football, twenty-five is good enough." We'd be in training camp and he'd catch the ball, sprint forty yards, and run into somebody on defense, just put his shoulder down and try to roll them. I'm like, "Jeremy, come on man, you're going to get them boys on defense all riled up. I'm tired, I'm hot, I don't feel like dealing with them today." To say he works hard is an understatement. He's always running hard. When he drops one, he punts the ball like forty or fifty yards. He gets so upset with himself when he drops the ball. He'll be like, "Man, I'm better than that. I'm better than that." I'm like, "Okay, if you want to play, go on to the next time and don't worry about it." But he stays all frustrated. "I'm better than that shit, man, I don't drop balls like that." It will be like two series behind us and he's still talking about it. He just hates to mess up, hates to drop a ball. That just says a whole lot about him. I'm like, "Chill out, we got a game on Sunday."

Shock works hard and he plays hard, too, if you know what I mean. The women, they all like him. It doesn't matter—black, white, Mexican, Brazilian, Japanese, Italian, German, it doesn't matter. They all love him. That says a lot about a man. That says a lot about him. It's because he's so open, so comfortable with who he is, totally unafraid. I know black girls who just love him. It's crazy. Yeah, he's a bad boy. Ain't nothing wrong with that. Good girls like bad guys. Anybody who would tell you that they wouldn't want to party with Jeremy Shockey, they're lying, they're not telling the truth. If they like to go out and party and hang out, they would love to go party and hang with this guy.

From South Florida to the Bahamas? Oh man, oh man, you are shorting him a couple countries. You're talking about Panama, Colombia, Brazil, Canada. He's everywhere. I can't even keep tabs on him. He'll call me when he has a layover in the States or something. He'll be like, "Hey, man, what's going on?"

I'm like, "Damn, man, where you been?"

"I've been in Panama for a month," he says.

"For a month? What you doing now?"

"I'm in Texas, man, I'm about to catch a flight to Brazil."

"All right, man, how long are you going to be over there?"

"I don't know, I'll call you when I get back." Gone. I'll hear from him in about another three or four weeks. It's just how it is. World traveler, loves to do it. He's single, girls love him, why not take advantage and have fun? If I was single, hmm, I'd still be rolling, hard. But that's not the case with me anymore. That's far from the case with me now. It's like Shock calls me and says, "Hey, you got to go hang with your boys sometimes." I'm like, "Jeremy, how am I going to go hang with you? What am I going to do? Walk upstairs and ask Tiffany, can I go to Brazil for a few days with you? How do you think that's going to fly?" He says, "You're right, bro. I'm never getting married." He's hilarious. He's out of control, having fun. It's going to be four in the morning, if he even makes it in. But, like I said, when it's time to play on Sunday, it's time to play and he's going to be there.

We got some other characters on the team. Sam Madison just won his first Super Bowl after eleven years in the league. I was so happy for him. The smile on his face, priceless. He's one of the great trash talkers in the league, the kind of guy who gets me fired up if I was playing against him. I've never seen a guy who's always so good like him. He's all-time. He got Carolina Pro Bowl wide receiver Steve Smith so hot one game. We were playing Carolina in 2006 and he talked Steve right out of his game. He got Steve so upset with the trash that he was talking. Steve was trying to beat him on plays when the ball wasn't even coming his way. Sam was just tiring him out, making him run every play. Sam would be grabbing him, roughing him outside, and Smith is yelling at the refs, looking for a call. Sam would say, "Stop crying, you've got to be vigilant." They got into it. Then, at halftime, they talked trash from the field to the locker room. Sam is walking with Steve all the way to Carolina's locker room, still talking. Finally, we yell at Sam, "Yo, over here" and he's like, "Oh, gotta go." Even during training camp, Sam is feisty. He's one of the best talkers I've ever been around. And he ain't talking nice, either. He'll say something bad about you. He'll get personal. I got to like it because he's on my team.

Sam also has some tricks. His best move is you get him at the two-minute drill and the receiver got to get up real fast. Sam is going to lay on you. He's going to make you push him off and he'll roll back the other way and stay on you a little longer. The receiver is crying, "Hey, get him off me," and Sam is saying, "What'd I do, what did I do?" The receiver is running back and his whole team is like waiting for him, yelling at him to get moving. Sam is famous for that now. He's got everybody on our team doing that. He's also one of the best holders I've been around. Sneaky, too. If you get an outside release on him, he wouldn't hold you because he knows the ref will see it. Instead, he'll just be restricting your thigh, patting on your thigh as you're trying to run so you can't get to top speed. He'll do it to me in practice and I'm like, "Sam, come on." He'll say, "I'm doing my job. I'm not going to let you make me look bad."

Strahan doesn't do much talking during games. He used to get mad if he was getting held in a game, but he doesn't do that as much now. But if Stray gets a couple of sacks, then he's talking. You hear him hollering, "Hey, I'm the best to ever do it. I broke all of Lawrence Taylor's records. I'm the best that ever was. You're in my house."

Like I said, I like the trash talk. It's all fun, just gets you going. Plus, if somebody talks to me, that just gets me motivated. So the trash talkers, I love to play against them. The guy I hated playing against was Aaron Glenn. He is just a pest and he's always trying to butter me up. Total opposite of a trash talker. Aaron would be like, "Hey, man, what's up?" I'm like, "Aaron, don't try that today, man. Don't try that shit, being my brother and all, and then take it to the house." But he just keeps going. He'll say, "Hey, man, they got to give you the ball more, man. If you're open, why don't they throw it to you?" Then he says, "It ain't easy covering you, man, you're so open. You gotta go to the sideline and say something to them boys, it ain't easy."

You look at Aaron on tape and he's the smallest guy on the football field, but you can't beat him. He'd be all in your hip pocket. If you go up here waiting for the ball, he'd come through here and just shoot through your body and deflect the ball. I'm saying, "Man, leave me the hell alone, get away from me." Just frustrating you. Terence Newman of Dallas is the same way. If you get open, it's never by more than half a step. Terence is never going to intercept a lot of balls, but he's not going to let you get too many, either.

Anyway, then you would catch a pass on Aaron and you're trying to make him miss, but he'll stand still and then he'd jump right through your feet at the last minute. He's got both of your feet like this and you'd be like, "Get off of me." Annoying, man. He'd tackle you in open field and you go back to the sideline and the coach is saying, "It's third-and-seven, I would have put my money on you with that one." You get in the meeting the next day and the coach says it again, "I would have put my money on you against that guy every single time. That little guy is a fool." I'm like, "Man, I'm telling you, it ain't that easy playing against that dude." He's just always pestering you. I'm six foot five playing against a guy five foot seven and I never could get open. I never could really beat him.

He was so smart, man, and he was so quick. That's how he was still playing last year after fourteen years. He was with Dallas the first two years after I got to New York. He's pretty strong, too. He don't back down for nothing. But he would never talk shit. Never. And he wouldn't let me talk shit, either. I'd tell him to shut up and he'd say, "Hey, hey, hey, I'm trying to help you out. Why are you telling me to shut up?" Trying to help me out, my ass. He's a great player, though. He'd always get a pick, too. Every time I played against him, he would intercept that ball. When I was with Pittsburgh and we played Houston one time when he was there, he intercepted two. When I broke, he was always right there. He would just jump in front of me. Did it twice. He did the same thing to me my first year with the Giants. I learned that on the slant route, he'd undercut me for a pick. The first time, I ended up tackling him back at the twenty. Then the bastard did it again. I'd just look at him and think, How does he keep picking up all these balls from me?

He even got us in 2006. We got down to the five-yard line, and he backed off. I got a slant route, but he's intercepted like three slant routes that I know of over my time. So the ball is hiked, and I run like I'm going to the fade route to the outside. My head is turning that way and he struts out. Then I put my right foot down and I run the slant and nobody is there to cover me, but Eli never threw the ball. Eli threw the ball to Jeremy in the corner for the touchdown. But I'm wide open and Aaron is like, "Hey, that was a good move. Great move." Buttering me up again, just like that. So we get down to the end zone again. So this time I got the same route on, playing again on my right-hand side. So I'm giving him the same move, but I try to give him a little skip and a shake to sell the fade a little better. When I tell you I jumped up to give him a little shake, he was gone. He knew it was a slant and just jumped and I'm like, *Oh no*. Lucky me, he dropped it. He hit the ground and just yelled, "No!" He would have had a touchdown. It would have been a ninety-five-yard return. I was so relieved that we got the chance to kick a field goal because he was gone, nobody would have even touched him.

Coaches have a list of the guys at corner that if you throw it in their direction and they get their hands on it, they're going to catch it. He's one of them. The other one who will catch is Dré

Bly. There's only five guys like that. Aaron Green is the best since I've been in the league. Most cornerbacks are just little receivers who can't catch. They think they can, but they can't. It's like Will Allen who used to be with the Giants and is in Miami now. He can cover, but if the ball is in front of him, he can't catch it. It's like, "Man, what's going on with your hands?"

Making Some Changes

A couple of days after the end of the 2006 season, we all got the news that Coughlin was coming back for the next season. He had a bunch of meetings with the owners and Jerry Reese before they made the decision, so I guess they talked about him changing his attitude and everything, which he did a little bit. Again, that's fine by me. Whether he's the coach or if it's somebody else doesn't affect what I have to do as a player. As players, our job is to play our asses off. And when I got the news, it really wasn't the biggest thing going on in my life. I think they announced it on a Wednesday. Me and Tiffany were getting ready for her to have the baby. We had more important stuff to deal with.

But we got everything settled, I had surgery, and after a couple of months it was time to start thinking about the next season. The biggest thing about Coughlin coming back was that he made some changes to the staff. John Hufnagel had been the offensive coordinator the year before, but Tom replaced him with Kevin Gilbride, who had been the quarterbacks coach working with Eli. Hufnagel called the plays the year before, with Tom getting involved sometimes. I guess Tom just didn't think he was the right guy at that point. As far as I was concerned, I never really had much of a relationship with Hufnagel, so it didn't really matter. I knew Gilbride from when I was in Pittsburgh, so that was fine. He was one of my offensive coordinators there, so he knew me and what I could do. The other thing that happened was they brought in Chris Palmer to replace Gilbride as the quarterbacks coach. Palmer was a really experienced guy, too, so that had to help. They told me that they were going to change the offense, the terminology and stuff.

The year before, I didn't come to New York at all for the off-season program, even though Eli said he wanted me and Jeremy Shockey to be there. Like I said, I just don't think we need to do all that work and I'm working out in South Florida to be ready. I need the rest, but I'm going to take care of myself and be ready. But this year was different. With Gilbride taking over as offensive coordinator and Chris Palmer coming in, I needed to be there so I could be on the same page with Eli in the off-season. So I came back in May and part of June. What I said at the time was, "For me, it means a lot the older I get, the more that I play in this league. Just trying to improve on little things that we didn't do so well last year . . . I'm not trying to make a statement. I'm just here because I want us to be better and I want [Manning] to reach his full potential, which I think can be great. I feel I'm one of the best players in the world at my position. If it takes me to come back and work with my quarterback right now to get to that level, then I'm more than willing to do that because I believe I can be that person." I still really couldn't run routes or anything because my ankle was healing, but just learning the new terminology and doing it with Eli there was important.

Anyway, I headed back to South Florida to work on my ankle to strengthen it. I was working with Joe Caroccio and Pete

Bommarito at Perfect Competition. Joe has me doing all these drills to strengthen my left ankle and he was working on my right ankle, too. We were doing these toe lifts where I was shifting my weight around to different parts of my foot to strengthen my foot and ankle. At the time I didn't understand why he was working on my right ankle, too. I thought, *Why do I have to do this?* But I realized after the season how important it was. With Pete, I couldn't really run yet and I didn't want to run as much in the off-season as I had the previous year. But we started doing this sled drill. You put a harness around your waist and they attach a sled with weights on it behind you. You don't run, but you plant your heel and then roll onto the front of your foot, so it's the same motion as running and you're working the same muscles. You just don't have the pounding on your joints. At that point, I couldn't run with my ankle the way it was and I didn't want to wear out my body. I wanted to be fresh and well rested for the season. The funny part is that I was doing great with the sled. I was just killing the other guys out there, except for Fred Taylor. Fred is so competitive. I beat him one day and he was fussing like mad. The rest of the guys, like Byron Leftwich, I'm just lapping them. Some of those guys are even throwing up. You pull this thing on the grass or on a rubber track out in the sun.

We started training camp. I was not ready to go at all. I was going to practice, one a day every other day. Coughlin had no choice. I just had surgery on my ankle and it was not healing as fast as anticipated. You couldn't put me on the field when it's not right. He wasn't really someone I go up and talk to about a situation. We didn't have too much interaction.

But right from the first day of training camp, me and Gilbride hit it off. Again, I'd known him a long time, so I knew what I could say and what not. We got on each other, cracking jokes on each other. I got on him 'cause he went to Southern

Connecticut State. I was like, "Man, where is that at? Is that even a college?" We got to have a lot of fun this year in the classroom and on the field. We both had a positive attitude toward each other. We became close friends, he's somebody I can really trust. I can go talk to him. We sit down and have conversations all the time now.

He is a good man. I mean, I can tell that he wants the best for me, and when somebody wants the best for you, you kind of open to him a little bit more, take your wall down, so to speak. For example, there was a time when I was late two days in a row for treatment. He pulled me to the side and said, "Hey, I don't want people to start looking at you and start judging you another way. As a friend, just try to get here on time so you don't have to deal with things inside." It's just a little thing like that that let me know that maybe some things were being said and he came to me, man-to-man, and said just try to get here on time so you can quiet everything down. It's things like that. He's not ordering me, he's helping me understand, and everybody is more receptive when you can talk to them as a person, when you can talk like we are all on the same level. Not like, "I'm the coach and you're the player and you do what I say or else." We're all much more receptive as players and people when we're talked to all on the same level.

People don't have to fuss at me or tell me what I'm doing wrong. I already know what I'm doing wrong. I've been playing this game going on nine years. It's like that in meetings with me and Gilbride. He doesn't even talk to me like he's correcting. He'll just say, "What happened here?" and have me explain it back to him, and then he moves on to the next player. By doing that with me, he can show everybody that me and him have an open relationship. It makes it so much easier for all the receivers and everybody on the offense. If I'm, so to speak, the go-to guy on the offense and we can talk like that, it opens it up to communicate with everybody. Now everybody can kind of get on that level with everybody else. He can say to Steve Smith, "What do you think you did here?" and not have it be all intimidating. He doesn't have to stop the tape and fuss and cuss. He asks them, "What do you think you did wrong?" and it's a conversation. That's what happened this year. If it wasn't good he would say it wasn't good. He wouldn't get to the point where he would flat-out embarrass you. Like to me, sometimes he'd just look at the tape and say, "Seventeen, whoever that is, this is not good." Then he would go on to the next player. He doesn't have to explain it to me, but he'd get his point across and we would actually start busting up in the meeting. It was his little way of joking on me and then lighten up the room for everybody. Then, at the end of the meeting, he'd come up to me and say something like, "You know what I was saying, you are so fast and so strong, trust yourself."

Anyway, for me training camp up in Albany, New York, was pretty boring. I would rehab during the day and then, just to keep it fun, I would do things I wouldn't normally do. Maybe break curfew just to break it 'cause I didn't want it to be totally boring. Maybe we'd go to a bar like early. Then we'd go back for bed check and tell everybody, "Hey, we'll be right back." Look, I can't practice when I'm hurt. I might as well try to enjoy myself and have a little bit of fun. At one point, Mike Garafolo of the *Newark Star-Ledger* told me that one of my teammates thinks I'm milking my ankle injury, just riding the bike every day. Mike didn't say who it was, but I trusted him. He wouldn't bullshit me, so I said, "It's fine. But when I get back on the football field, when I get back out there and back to being number seventeen and making plays, everybody's going to shut up and get in line." I didn't play the entire preseason, not a single down. I was paying close attention so I'd know what I was supposed to do. The thing about it is, after so many years, I don't really have to run the routes, but I have to pay attention to the timing, how other people are running the routes. I can get the mental reps in my head. I just have to focus and I was doing that.

The other supposedly big story of training camp was Michael Strahan holding out. He was talking about retiring and all this stuff, but we all knew what was going on. He didn't want to go to training camp. I can't blame him for that. Training camp is too long anyway. Look, the way the league is now, players have all this off-season training. Either we're with the team all off-season or we're working out on our own to stay in shape. Anybody who doesn't work out in the off-season isn't going to last very long in the league now. Training camp isn't about getting in shape. If a guy's not in shape in training camp, he's probably getting cut. Camp is about getting ready for the season. Really, we need two or three games and maybe four weeks of practice to be ready for the season. So when people were flipping out about Strahan not being there, they just didn't get it. Here's a guy with fifteen years' experience, he's a Hall of Famer for sure. What do you think he's going to get out of training camp except tired? He's going to be in shape.

He always is and he has too much pride to come in looking bad. That's just not him, although when he showed up with that beard, we were sort of wondering what's going on with that. But people were still freaking, wondering what we all are thinking about him not being around. We broke camp and it's the week before the season and he showed up. It was all cool.

So the regular season came and we opened up at Texas Stadium. I wasn't disturbed by the Dallas game at all. When we can go down to Texas Stadium and put up thirty-five points, we'll win those football games most of the time. The problem is, they scored forty-five. Even with the defense, there wasn't much to get discouraged about by the Dallas game. It was the first time our defense played as a unit. They were learning a whole new defensive scheme under new defensive coordinator Steve Spagnuolo, who took over when Coughlin fired Tim Lewis after the 2006 season. There were guys who didn't understand what they were doing at that point, but you knew they were going to get it. There were like five or six passes over twenty yards they were giving up. I was just thinking, *Hey, if y'all can just slow them down for a drive, maybe we can come out with a win.* It didn't happen, but we weren't really discouraged.

It's funny, the Cowboys don't talk a lot of trash. They don't want to get me riled up. You know their secondary is not that good anyway. Terence Newman is a good player and I like Kenny Hamlin. But outside of them, there's not much. Now, the Cowboys' game is always physical and tough, especially at Texas Stadium. They're a whole different team playing at Texas Stadium. Get them on the road and they're a pretty average team. Anyway, I'm having a monster game. I finished with nine catches, 144 yards, and three touchdowns. So I'm trying to talk some trash to them. At some point in the game, I've got two touchdowns already and it's a TV time-out. I see Hamlin over there and I go, "Hey, man, you were on a roll last year, but all that shit changed. I'm running through y'all's secondary like shit through a tin horn." He doesn't say nothing, so I said, "Hey, Kenny, come here, man, let me talk to you." But the time-out was ending, so he just looked over at me and he said, "You ain't even in my top ten fantasy players." That was classic. That was hilarious. It was so funny we both busted out laughing. That was a classic line, man. It was so funny I told my teammates about it on the sideline. I had no comeback or nothing.

The other thing about that game to me was that we were really on the right track on offense. It's not just that I had a big game, but we were doing some things that were pretty special. We had this one touchdown where I was double-covered on the play. It was a bracket coverage with Jacque Reeves on the outside and safety Roy Williams in the middle. Newman was to my outside and had the fade covered. Roy Williams was sitting right there taking away the slant. I mean just sitting there, not even trying to fake the coverage. But the way they had it set up, I had to run the slant. I kind of ran a banana route instead of doing it straight and I saw that Roy wasn't even moving. I was running from right to left now. I was three steps into the route and I just threw my right hand up in the air to signal to Eli where to throw it. Eli threw it so perfect that Roy couldn't even react as it went right over his right shoulder. I mean, it was right there in the only spot where he could get it because Roy should have taken the whole thing away. I think Roy was just shocked that Eli even tried it. That's sort of Roy's mentality. I think he's a defensive lineman playing safety. He's good, but not like the LaRon Landrys, Sean Taylors, Ed Reeds, or Troy Polamalus. He's not one of them. He gets all the pub, though. After we got to the sideline, Gilbride came over and he apologized for making that call against that defense, but he told us, "You guys outplayed the call."

Eli hurt his shoulder in the Dallas game. Looked pretty bad at first and the talk was he might miss five or six weeks. He showed a lot of toughness. Between how he reacted to Tiki Barber's criticism and how he handled the injury—didn't say shit, just played—I think guys really appreciated that. I knew he wasn't good, but he never said anything about it. Nobody wanted to hear it anyway. He was back out there for the Green Bay game. The big thing about how Eli handled the whole Tiki thing is that he didn't blow the whole thing up like the media was doing. Eli said what he thought and let it go right there. He couldn't handle it any better and it was over for the players. I don't know if those guys ever talked, but Eli stood up for himself without making a big deal out of it.

Now, the Green Bay game was different. I remember losing that game and I just thought we were so much better than those guys and we got whipped. With everything that happened, me getting hurt and we couldn't move the ball, that was one of the worst losses I've had. But I'm still thinking at the end of the game, Man, we are so much better than them and we got whipped. That really played on my head a lot. We looked at it on tape and we started out pretty cool on offense and then the second half was just horrible. I ended up leaving the game in the third quarter and then they just kind of ran away with it. Brett Favre was slinging the ball all over the place. But I remember saying at the end of that game, the only way we should play that team again is in the NFC Championship. We wanted to play them again really bad. They had some guys talking serious trash. Linebacker Nick Barnett was talking so much trash. I was like, Who is this guy talking all that trash? When we played them the next time, I remembered everything that happened the first game, how Johnny Jolly, A. J. Hawk, and Cullen Jenkins were talking so much trash. They were saying all this stuff and it was like, who are these guys? I don't know none of these guys.

The big problem for me in this game is that I get hurt. First, on the second play of the game, Al Harris grabbed my hand as I went to block him on a running play and I snapped the tendon in my left pinkie. It was the same injury that Kobe Bryant played with this season. The trainers wanted to tape my fingers together to give it support, but I didn't want to do that to the rest of my hand. I still can't ball my left hand into a fist with that finger, but I can still catch, so I'm not going to have surgery on it. Then I hurt my right ankle and that was a big deal. I had first aggravated the ankle back in the beginning of training on August 2. It was just sore for most of training camp, but it wasn't like some big deal. In the second quarter of the Green Bay game, though, Harris stepped on my right foot as I started to make a cut and I could hear the pop in my foot. He wasn't doing it intentionally or anything, but he stepped on my foot and I was like, "Oh shit, I just tore something." It was so sore right away. Sure enough, I came into the locker room and said something was wrong with my ankle. I tried to come out in the third quarter, but I lasted one series and I couldn't go back in. We couldn't do anything the rest of the game and the Packers beat us 35–13. Here we were at 0–2 and everybody was freaking out in New York. The media was saying we're done already.

Fact is, I almost thought *I* was done, too.

13

Playing Without Practice

ootball people have been saying for a hundred years that
you can't just walk out there and play in this game; any
game really. Coaches always talk about how there is no substi-
tute for practice and you have to get your reps. But after the
Green Bay game in the regular season, I couldn't practice.
The funny part is that I scored a touchdown in that game, so
now I had four touchdowns in the first two games. But, oh
man, was I in pain. I was limping around because my ankle
was hurting so bad and my teammates were like, it's not that
bad, you just scored two touchdowns. They didn't know about
my injury. In fact, they didn't know anything about it until
the end of the season because I couldn't say anything about
how bad it really was.

Now we're in the third week, we were getting ready to play
at Washington, but I didn't practice. The guys were saying, you
just don't want to practice. But I was so sore and just hoping my
ankle would be good enough so I could go on Sunday. I still didn't
know exactly what was wrong with my ankle. I knew something
was torn, that it was a really bad sprain. What it turned out to
be was a torn deltoid ligament. It was off the bone. The deltoid

is there to keep the foot from rolling outward when you cut. Most sprains occur when you roll your ankle the other way and the heel of your foot points inward and tears the ligaments on the outside of the foot. But when you have a deltoid ligament tear, it's really painful and you can't keep steady on your cuts.

The night before we played Washington, receivers' coach Mike Sullivan had a friend of his come in to talk to us. It was Lieutenant Colonel Greg Gadson, who played with Sully at Army when they were in college. Gadson had just gotten back from Iraq, where he lost both his legs and hurt his arm in a bombing. He was pretty amazing to listen to and we gave him a big ovation after. He just kept telling us how preparation was the key to his life. He prepared for battle and he prepared for what might happen. He just kept saying, if you don't prepare, you can't succeed when you start facing the challenges, when it gets difficult. I told this to the reporters later, "I never met a guy in his condition who was in such high spirits. When you see people like that, you kind of say to yourself, 'Man, all I have is an ankle injury.'" For the rest of the season, Gadson was around here and there. He was one of the captains at the Green Bay playoff game and then he went to the Super Bowl with us.

So, back to the Washington game. I didn't think they were taking us that seriously. After the game, I told the reporters, "In the back of their minds they already had us beat. If you turned on the TV before the game, you realized that all the things that they were saying were like they were just going to walk on top of us. They didn't think that we were a good football team." But the game wasn't going that good from the start. I dropped two balls in the first half, including a deep one, and Eli had a rough time. He got sacked and fumbled and the Redskins scored a touchdown. Then he got intercepted just before halftime and they got a field goal. They're up 17–3 on us and it's like we've been playing from behind all season. We gave up seventy-seven points in the first two games and now we're giving up more and the offense isn't helping. But we came back in the second half and got a drive to get within a touchdown and then we tied it with another drive in the fourth quarter. Now our defense was coming up big, stopping the Redskins cold. With about eight minutes left, Antonio Pierce came up with a fumble recovery. We drove and then Eli hits me with a short pass.

I don't know how I did it, but I made a move on Carlos Rogers and then Sean Taylor and got in the end zone for a thirty-three-yard touchdown to go up 24–17 with about five minutes left. Before I say anything else about the game, I just want to talk about Sean T. for a second. I went to his funeral later that year and that was so sad. The other thing is that Sean was like a lot of us. People didn't know who he really was away from the field and a lot of people drew conclusions about him from how he played or from a few stories that came out about him, run-ins with bad people, stuff like that. But he was a personable man, so outgoing, loved playing video games, just so humble. I mean really humble. He was two totally different people, the football-field person and the off-the-field person.

The way he played, you'd have thought he was crazy. The way he played the game, he played it reckless. He only knew one way to play it and that was all out for sixty minutes. I said this when I did the ESPN 60 thing and they asked me several questions. One of these questions was, name one person on the field that you gotta know where they are at? I had like five seconds to answer, and I said Sean Taylor. This was before he passed away. They said, "Why do you say that?" And I told them that if you don't know where this guy is, he will take your helmet off. That was just exactly how he played. I always made sure I knew where 21 was because if you didn't know where he was, he was going to let you know.

But off the field, man, you wouldn't even believe it was the same person. He was cool, a super-humble man. I'd see Sean, and it would be like ten or eleven at night, and ask if he wanted to go get something to eat and then go party and hang out. We'd be riding down South Beach with some of my friends and we'd ask him, but he would always say, "Oh, man, I'm on my way to go work out." That was his thing, when everybody else was resting or partying, he was working.

Anyway, we got the lead and then the defense really pumped it up on the final two drives by the Redskins. First, they got to our thirty-five-yard line, but Justin Tuck and Mathias Kiwanuka sacked Jason Campbell, who fumbled, and all of a sudden they were out of field-goal range and had to punt. Then came the final drive and this one probably got us going as much as anything all season. Washington got to a first-and-goal at our one-yard line after we almost gave up a touchdown on a pass from Jason Campbell to Antwaan Randle El. We're thinking we might have to play overtime. Washington spikes the ball on first down to stop the clock 'cause they're out of time-outs. Then they throw an incomplete pass. Then on third and fourth down, our defense stopped them cold at the line. It was just awesome. We got a win. For me, I had gotten five touchdowns in three games and that became a pretty big deal for the rest of the season as I dealt with this injury.

We got back to New York and my right ankle wasn't feeling any better. I was really in a lot of pain, so I told the Giants I wanted to get a second opinion and have my agent set it up so I can see Dr. Anderson in Charlotte. Me and Giants trainer Ronnie Barnes flew down there and I met with the doctor. He basically explained to me the whole deal with the ligament and kind of laid out how I could handle it. My options were put it on the shelf and get surgery, which I didn't really want to do after having surgery on the other ankle a few months before that. The other thing I could do is have him put it in a boot for six weeks and see if it healed. The doctor said that might not work, and if I did that, my leg was definitely going to be weak when it got out of the cast. So I didn't really want to do that, either. Or he said I could just play with it and not practice. He was telling this to me and Ronnie while Coughlin and Jerry Reese were on the speakerphone. Coughlin didn't like hearing the no-practice idea, but it was what the doctor was saying, so he really couldn't argue with it. So we decided I'd try it again this week and just not practice. The doctor said I couldn't make it any worse than it already was. I was just going to be sore. Look, as long as the GM and coaches understood the deal, then I wouldn't have to fight with them about it. I said I'd give it a go.

Then I played in the Philadelphia game and I got only four catches for twenty-four yards. The problem wasn't my totals. We won the game and the defense was just amazing. We got twelve sacks and Osi Umenyiora got six by himself. That game was easy for the offense. The problem I had was that I couldn't move. I couldn't cut, I was sore as hell, it was just bad. I couldn't get off the line and the only thing saving me was I had five touchdowns already, so the defense was playing off me. If they knew, they would have just come to the line and jammed me all game. There was no way I could get away from the defender. If he played me bump-and-run, I'd be exposed, but they were scared to do it right now. I had one play where Quinton Mikell overpowered me and another where I made a nice move on Sheldon Brown, but I couldn't sprint past him.

The other thing is that my timing with Eli wasn't good then. Coughlin told the reporters that week, "Yeah, that's what you worry about because you don't have the chance to work your way through that stuff [in practice] and you don't get caught in those situations [when] the two of them can eyeball each other and walk up and talk about it. It happens on game day and, at that point in time, things are happening so fast it's difficult—until you come to the sidelines—to even be able to work it out." Even I had to admit that was part of the problem. "I'm not as crisp as I want to be, as sharp as I want to be. Just physically, your judgment on the ball might be a little off. You're not used to running full speed and catching all at the same time" is what I said then.

So that week I went into Reese's office. I was so frustrated. I couldn't move and I was thinking that I just wanted to shut it down, get the surgery on the ankle, and get this thing fixed. Jerry looked at me and said, "But you already have five touchdowns and you're off to the best start of your career." I told him again how frustrated I was, but then he gets down to it and says, "Plaxico, we need you." So I thought about it some more. The thing is that the doctors and the coaches know I'm not pulling their chain. We couldn't say anything to the media or the players right now, but they knew and they were telling me it was okay to not practice, to save myself for Sunday and just do whatever. If I could continue to draw some double-teams and get other guys open, that's all they needed.

The whole thing with not telling anybody, it was kind of a double-edged sword. If I played horrible, you know, it would have been, "Oh, he's hurt, he's giving it a try." It would have been so easy to make an excuse. Then if I went out and did what I did, everybody would be like, "Oh, he is jerking us around. He's not hurt, he's just not practicing." But the Giants couldn't tell anyone what the deal was or the other teams would know how to defend me. They couldn't tell the truth.

I didn't expect to do anything. I was just expecting to go out and draw some double coverage and open some things up for other guys. But what happened is I learned a lot about myself and the game. I learned so much about myself this past year it's crazy.

The ankle started off being injured on the inside part of the foot. To keep it from popping all the time and getting really painful, they would turn my foot as far as they could turn it inward, so that the outside edge of the foot looked like the blade of an ice skate, and then tape it in place like that. Then they would put a support in my shoe to keep my foot in place like that as much as possible once I put my shoe on. I played with my foot like this for thirteen weeks. By doing that, I ended up spraining the outside part of the foot, too, but I figured I'd just deal with that.

And I was on so many medications I really couldn't feel my foot until Monday. I would come in on Monday and all that shit would wear off. It was so bad I couldn't even walk straight for the rest of the week. They never shot up my ankle, it was just pills. I'd go through Toradal, Indocin, and Aleve. I was just trying anything that would work.

I was taking a combination of medications. I wouldn't take the Indocin during the week because it was really hard on my stomach. I only took one of those a week because it's so strong. I would take Toradal and Aleve during the week. Then, at midnight on Saturday, I would take the Indocin and then they would put a patch with medicine on my ankle and I would sleep with that on. It was like a big Band-Aid with medicine in it. Then, about three hours before the game, I would take more medication. It would take away some of the pain and usually about halftime of every game I started to feel good. I was always better in the second half of games. Then come Monday, and it was back to being sore as hell.

That's where I found out so much about myself. I couldn't practice, but I had to find a way to keep up with what I was supposed to know. That's where I looked at guys like Rodney Harrison, Derrick Brooks, and Junior Seau. All those guys have been playing so long.

Strahan, too. Are any of those guys as good as they used to

be physically? No, there's no way. You can't take that kind of beating and still be as quick and as strong as you used to be. But what keeps them at the top of their game is they're so smart and they maximize their work. My thing this season was, I didn't practice the game, but I played the game.

There is a difference between practicing the game and playing the game. I played the game and I love to play it. I just had to find a way to get a step or two ahead or I wouldn't have been able to do a thing. I watched so much film this year. I was in my playbook so much, taking notes, knowing when I was supposed to be the hot receiver, paying attention in practice to all the little things. Now that I've worked that into my game, I can't wait to get back on the field this year. This year, the 2008 season, coming up.

I can't wait till the season starts and I'm 100 percent.

The other thing that happened as the season went on is that Gilbride was talking to me constantly about what was going on. We'd come off the field right after the first series. It was me, Eli, Gilbride, and the other receivers and they'd say, "How's your guy playing you? What do you want to do?" So I would say that I had this guy sitting behind me and a guy in the slot, and, hey, if they are going to play me like that, then I could line up over here and then another receiver would be wide open. It wouldn't be me just drawing plays for myself. It would be me and Amani and the other receivers talking about how the other team was defending us. Hey, if you used me as bait to take out a defender and let somebody else be wide open, that works. That's how it's supposed to be. We're talking and the coaches are saying, "All right, I'll get someone to look at it upstairs in the coaching booth." I draw plays for Jeremy to get him open. Maybe run a double post and make the defense make a choice about who they want to cover. All sorts of stuff, but it's about talking. In 2006, we never had that with Hufnagel. He'd just call the plays and he didn't talk to too many of us. It was a lot of fun this year. We didn't have a whole lot of bickering about who was getting the ball. We had so many guys making plays that nobody complained.

That was just our attitude. When I was over there getting doubled-teamed and Amani was doing his thing, I got so much joy when we came to the sidelines, just to see how happy everyone got when they were getting their touches. It made me feel good.

Anyway, I was playing through this injury. Against the Jets, we fell behind again 17–7 in the first half. The Jets got a fumble recovery for a touchdown. Then they got a kick return in the second half. Our defense was really doing a good job; we just let a couple of plays get away. As we'd talked about earlier in the week, the Jets double-teamed me early on in the game. They knocked away a deep one that I almost got. They were just doing everything they could to take me away. This time, it was helping our running game because the Jets weren't playing with an eighth guy in the box, so Brandon Jacobs and Derrick Ward were gashing them. After a while the coaches came to me and said, let's work some individual stuff to the weak side of the formation.

So we eventually had the Jets stacked up on the run and they got me one-on-one with Andre Dyson. Eli threw me a quick hitch, I juked Dyson, stayed in bounds, and got a fifty-three-yard touchdown. That play almost never happens in the NFL. That was the go-ahead touchdown and then Aaron Ross sealed it with an interception return for a touchdown. I now had seven touchdowns in five games. More important, we had three wins in a row after beating the Jets 35–24. Playing the Jets isn't really a big rivalry game. It's more about bragging rights for the city of New York and about whose stadium it really is. Like it says on the outside, it's Giants Stadium.

Then the next three games our defense kicked it in and we

beat San Francisco, Atlanta, and Miami. Those teams weren't real good and none of them scored more than fifteen points, and now we're at 6–2 and feeling pretty good. The game against Miami was in London. It was cool to go over there. Tiffany had a pretty good line in the *New York Times*. She said, "If he has a great game and the crowd loves him, he'll say: 'You know what? I do like London.'"

Playing in Wembley Stadium was awesome. Great place. This was my first time going to Europe and the sites were cool, going to Big Ben and stuff like that. But we were so busy we didn't get a chance to do a whole lot of sightseeing. Some of it was ridiculous. We left on Thursday night at 6 P.M. and it's like a six-hour time difference. So we end up getting there at 7 A.M. and Coughlin says, we've got practice at 9:30 A.M. We were like, "Are you serious?" Guys hadn't even really had a chance to sleep and they had to go practice? Getting to practice was an hour-long bus ride. Man, that practice was ridiculous. I didn't have to practice because I was resting, so all I tried to do was fall asleep on the equipment cart. But the other guys were just dragging. I couldn't believe we tried to practice that morning. The food was bad, but it was cool to go over there. It was raining the whole time and it was cold, so you couldn't really enjoy it. We stayed one extra day after the game, but it was pouring, so we couldn't even go out. But the best thing was we had the bye week after that, so I could finally really rest my ankle for a week or so.

Like I said, we were all feeling pretty good. At least *we* were. Everybody in the media was talking about how this is the same time of the season last year where we fell apart. The week after we got back, I did a little practicing and the guys were riding me. I wasn't really going at it that hard, but after I caught the first ball in practice, all my teammates started clapping. That was pretty funny. They were riding me pretty good, but I was just trying to get in a groove again. Next day, I was back on the bike, resting.

We played Dallas and we hung with them for the first half. It was tied at seventeen, but then Terrell Owens got two touchdowns in the second half and we couldn't move the ball that well. Jeremy had a great game with twelve catches for 129 yards, but we couldn't get touchdowns, not like the first time we played them. They double-covered me almost the entire game and took away all the receivers, really. We still felt like we could move the ball against them when we had to, but we just weren't clicking and lost 31–20.

After the Dallas game, we got to Detroit and beat them guys pretty easily 16–10 to get to 7–3. We kept everybody quiet for a week, but then it got bad again after the Minnesota game. I don't know what it is about that team, but it's the second time in three years that they just killed us. Back in 2005, my first year with the Giants, the Vikings came to New York and Eli threw four interceptions. Next to the Carolina playoff game, that Vikings game was the worst of the season. Even with all the interceptions, we should have won, but they returned one interception for a touchdown right at the beginning of the game when Eli was trying to throw to me. Then they returned a kickoff for a touchdown and then they returned a punt for a touchdown. They got a field goal at the end and beat us 24–21. That game was ridiculous.

Now, the 2007 game might be worse because Eli had a really tough game. Not only did he throw four picks against these boys again, but three of them were returned for touchdowns. I mean, how do you give up six return touchdowns in two games against a team and give up eight interceptions to them? That's ridiculous. But the fans were brutal in this one because Minnesota kicked our asses 41–17. I scored a late touchdown, but it ain't even that close. This was against a team we should be beating. I mean, we were a better team. They didn't even have Adrian Peterson in that game. He was still hurt. The thing I was worried about was that the coaches were getting worried because of the weather, so before that game I told the press, "We know the weather is going to get bad, but we still have to throw the ball. If we don't, guys are going to line up eight in the box and put pressure on our running game. We're going to air it out this week." That didn't turn out so good. I was sitting over there on the bench watching and I was just like, Wow, we're getting beat so bad, we can't even really say nothing. We never gave ourselves a chance offensively. Then we played Chicago and we couldn't throw because of the weather.

The New York media was all over us after the Minnesota game and it was worse because we were losing at home. The fans were booing us. It was just bad. That's going to happen, but it's up to us to fix it. I don't think the fans have to do anything different. What we have to do is change it ourselves. We gotta start winning at home.

Then we went to Chicago and Eli threw a pick on the first series to Brian Urlacher on a double in route with me and Jeremy. I was on the outside and Eli threw it right to Brian. We were like, "Oh shit." I walked to the sideline thinking, *Oh man.* I could tell Eli wasn't feeling real good about himself at this point. Then he threw another one later that Peanut Tillman intercepted on a ball toward me. But we just changed up the whole thing and started handing the ball to Derrick Ward. He ran for 154 yards with Brandon Jacobs hurting. We got in a running formation with two tight ends and one receiver and just pounded away. They had an undersized defense, so they just couldn't stop it. I was on the sidelines for most of the first half because Amani was the receiver in the one-receiver formation. I was over there just watching the game. Derrick just, whew, went down the football field on them. But we had to stay patient in that game. Chicago was up 16–7 halfway through the fourth quarter before Amani caught a touchdown and then we came back on the next drive with a touchdown by Reuben Droughns with 1:31 remaining.

Even though we won, the fans and the media weren't happy with Eli. He did a great job in the fourth quarter to lead us back. There was this one fifteen-yard pass he hit me with that was just perfect. We were in third-and-nine and I ran a glance route. If I went outside I had to fade, but if I went inside, I had to run the post. So I got the choice of running either route. So I was thinking to myself, it's third-and–nine, if I take this ball and go inside, the percentage of me going in and making a play are a lot higher than me going outside because the wind is blowing and it's raining a little bit. I'm just going to go inside and make it happen. Eli threw a beautiful ball down low, and I dove and caught it and rolled over on the three-yard line. Then we punched it in for the win.

Still, I knew Eli was down a little because he's hard on himself. He's thrown eight interceptions in the past four games. It's not like it's all his fault. I mean, I got people who come up to me around New York and say, "What's wrong with Eli?" Do people really understand how hard it is to be a quarterback? To me, it's the hardest position in football. Nothing else is even close. Think about it this way, a quarterback can line up with four receivers and one running back and each one of those five guys can have three or four things they have to do depending on what the defense does. Then Eli has to check the blocking schemes depending on what he sees up front. And it's all got to happen in a matter of seconds. When I start to explain it to people like that, they go, "Oh, I see." But people don't see how much Eli has learned, especially this year. Like I wrote about earlier, from what we started with in the off-season to where he was with this offense by the time we got to the Super Bowl was unbelievable. He just knew it cold.

After this game, me, Jeremy, Antonio Pierce, and Jessie Armstead, we jumped in a private plane and flew down to Miami for Sean Taylor's funeral. Sean was shot by burglars who broke into his house the Monday before the Redskins were going to play Buffalo and we were going to play the Bears, and he died on Tuesday morning (November 27) from blood loss. We were all stunned. Just really shook up. That was a rough week for a lot of guys because of Sean. I talked about what kind of player he was and a little about who he was as a person. I would run into him a lot in South Florida all the years I've been down there. Being that it was Sean and he was such a good guy, it freaked guys out. Something like that can happen so fast and you could be gone. We're football players and people look at us with jealousy. Usually the enemy is someone who doesn't like you just because they see you out or you drive a nice car or you got on jewelry or whatever it may be. Some people don't like you just because your financial status is better than theirs.

This was a bunch of kids who wanted some stuff. That's what I'm saying. Things like that just open my eyes even more to my situation, that I just got to take care of myself the best I know how. I can't relax for a minute. Who wants to live like that? Who wants to live in fear? Who wants to constantly, 24/7, be worrying about how I didn't lock my door or I didn't turn my alarm on. Who is walking behind me? Or I can't go here. I don't want to live like that. I can't even relax no more and just hang out in the comfort of my own home and spend time with my family. I want to live as close to a normal life as I can. I have several guns and I had them before Sean got killed—a long time before that. I can get to them with all the lights out, blindfolded. I can go get them in all situations.

Now that I have a child, that intensified it. Sean's murder made it worse because I'm going to defend my family under any circumstances. That's not even anything for me to think about. It's just going to be a reaction. I don't think about it when it comes to my family, seriously. I can make sure nobody is going to try to hurt my family. Me and my wife had the conversation about the guns, to make sure they are put in high places and that I don't keep them loaded. That I keep my ammunition and my guns in two totally different places. I have two guns that I can take apart myself and put back together. I know them backward and forward. I have to. I did all the training back in 2001 and 2002. It was a three-and-a-half-week course. In Florida, you can purchase as many guns as you want. The third time you purchase one, though, they run your information through a computer again to make sure you haven't had any recent felonies, DUIs, or any run-ins with the law or anything like that.

Sean's death made us all think about stuff like that. Sean was just such a good dude. Sometimes he would just show up. He wouldn't call or nothing. I'd be sitting in the house and all of a sudden hear a *tap, tap, tap* on the door and I'd be like, "Hey, man, what you doing over here?" He'd say, "Oh, just riding through." I'm thinking, his place was way down in South Miami, like forty-five minutes away. He'd pop up in the strangest places. That's just how he was. You'd call him and he'd say, "I'm in the Keys just relaxing and hanging out with the children." He wasn't a real big partyer from what I know. He had a party when he got drafted, but nothing else outside of that. He was passionate about the game. He gave it everything he had. That's how he played. It was like in the 2007 Pro Bowl when he leveled punter Brian Moorman of the AFC team. Everybody was like, "You come to the Pro Bowl in a different mind-set. It's the Pro Bowl, everybody is just chillin'." But that again makes you understand how he played. His mind-set was, "I know it's the Pro Bowl, but I don't get paid to say I get paid, I get paid to put them on the ground." He only knew one way to play. That play in the Pro Bowl personified him right there.

We got back after the funeral in Miami, which was on a Monday. It was rough for a lot of people. Now we had to get ready to play at Philadelphia. As always, I can't practice. It doesn't really matter against the Eagles, because I usually have a good game against them. I had the one bad game earlier in the season when I was struggling. But in my first two years, I went over 100 yards against them three out of four times in the regular season and then I had the two touchdowns against them in the playoffs last year. They try to handle me with Sheldon Brown a lot and that's not working, and I've handled Lito Sheppard since that Florida game in college. This game is more of the same. I get seven catches for 136 yards and the game-winning touchdown—a 20-yard catch on a crossing pattern. We always seem to dominate the Eagles, especially down in Philly. Still, the game is close and we win 16–13 when David Akers misses a fifty-seven-yard field goal that would have tied it at the end. The ball hit the upright. Got another win and another one on the road, our sixth in a row away from home.

Us winning on the road became a big story, especially in the playoffs, when we had to win three straight on the road to get to the Super Bowl. Overall, we set an NFL record with ten straight road wins. It was pretty interesting because a lot of the time we just didn't play that good at home. Like I said before, I love how demanding our fans are; they don't accept mediocrity. They want us to win and they want us to win now and big. We didn't win a whole lot at home this year, and when that happens, we get booed. I think it got to where it was kind of like when we got away from home it was like a comfort zone, nobody but us. We ain't going to get booed here. Hell, if we messed up we're going to get cheered. I don't know if the fans were holding 2006 against us, but maybe they didn't trust that we were any good.

When we played on the road, we played a lot more focused, with a lot more intensity.

It's like dealing with the noise on the road and everything, we have to be so honed in with the call, and we have to almost look the quarterback in his mouth when he's calling the play. Otherwise we won't understand or hear what he's saying because it's so loud. So we got to pay attention to every little detail. When I say focus, that's what it takes to stay alert. We can't focus on what's going on over on the side. We just got to pay attention to what's going on right here. If we don't, if we miss one word, then we'll screw up the whole play. So we really gotta know what's going on and just blank out everything else. Nobody really has to say anything to get guys to focus. We've all been playing together enough to know what to expect out of one another. It's like I go back to that Carolina playoff game at home after the 2005 season and the Philadelphia game after the 2006 season. It's not a good feeling losing playoff games, especially in the fashion that we lost both of them.

Saturday night, we're back home before the Washington game. We were sitting in a room having a meeting and then the meeting was over and we were getting ready to have chapel. Giants director of player development Charlie Way walked in, saying, "David, David [Tyree], come here." We were just sitting in there and Charlie said, "David's mom just had a heart attack. She's dead." I busted out crying. I went over to David. Imagine somebody coming and telling you something like that, just out of the blue, just out of left field, that your mom just had a heart attack and died. I just felt so bad for him. I cried because I knew the pain that he was going through.

He didn't come back until the New England game. But, man, was he huge when he came back, as everybody knows from the Super Bowl.

So we played Washington the next day at home and the

wind was just howling. We're trying to throw on them, but Eli couldn't really do anything in the wind. We probably just should have run a bunch, but we got behind 22–3 in the third quarter. Eli ended up completing eighteen of fifty-three passes. There was one throw to me where the ball just blew almost all the way to the other side of the field. Man, you can get some windy games at Giants Stadium, but this was ridiculous. If all that wasn't bad enough, Jeremy Shockey breaks his leg in the third quarter when he got rolled up on. That's brutal for Shock 'cause he wants it so bad and he plays so hard. He's so emotional and this has been one really tough couple of weeks. From Sean T. to Tyree's mom to Shockey being out for the season, it's not good.

With Shockey gone, it hurts and all, but Kevin Boss gets to play. He's a rookie, but I've been watching him since training camp and he catches everything. This boy is smooth and he showed it right away in this game when he caught a nineteen-yard touchdown. It wasn't enough to get us back in the game, but at least we got somebody who can play the position. Like Tyree, Boss was huge in the playoffs, especially the Super Bowl. Boss is from Oregon. Big dude, like six foot six, but you don't see him running and stumbling and falling over his feet. He's big and smooth. He's got incredibly soft hands. He don't drop too many balls. Like I said, he was good even in training camp. On the times when we brought in two tight ends, we'd just run behind Boss. He's a great blocker, physical, and then he can run routes. If you've got soft hands as a tight end, there's nothing else that we can ask you to do. He doesn't show a lot of emotion. He just gets in there and plays. We didn't know too much about him from a game standpoint, him going out and guys jumping in his face and being physical, but he handled all of that.

That was kind of our team attitude. We didn't get overwhelmed with the situation that we were in. We just approached every game like, "Okay, this is what we've got to do. We've got to execute. We've got to convert third downs and score touchdowns in the red zone." We didn't really get caught up in how big the game was. That's just our team attitude. Me? I push every game as being like practice. I think that's kind of rubbed off on our receivers a little. I tell our guys, "Hey, it's just like practice. You've just got some people in the stands and you are going to get tackled. Other than that, it's just like practice." That's the way you calm the young guys down. You make them look at it that way. "It's just practice, we've been doing this shit all year." We don't let playing on big stages affect us.

So we were 9–5 now after losing to Washington. Now we headed up to Buffalo. The weather was going to be brutal—raining, snowing, sleeting, and the wind blowing like thirty-five miles per hour. It was freezing and nobody could throw the football. I had one catch for six yards. But we got a chance to get into the playoffs and we took it. It was a little scary for three quarters, but we won 38–21. The Bills came out really hyped because Kevin Everett walked on the field before the game. He'd been paralyzed in the opener. He was still struggling, but it was amazing to see him walking. Buffalo got out to a 14–0 lead and they were playing an eight-man front to take away our running game.

But our running game was smashing them all day. Brandon Jacobs was going strong. He got 143 yards on twenty-five carries and was looking good after the injuries he had earlier in the season. He was just a beast. A beast. He scored two touchdowns in the second quarter and we got the lead. They took it back in the third quarter, but then our defense came up big in the fourth quarter and we got a good look at Ahmad Bradshaw, out secret-weapon rookie. That's the game where our offensive line and the running game really all came together, totally complete. We were good before, but now we were good *and* explosive. When everybody knows you are going to run it and you can still run it, the other team is in trouble.

Still, the game was close until the fourth quarter, when we got three big plays and put the game away. First, Kawika Mitchell intercepted a pass and returned it twenty yards for a touchdown. Then our defense kept stopping them until Bradshaw broke an eighty-eight-yard run. That kid can fly and he runs really hard, as people got to see in the playoffs. He's a tough kid. I was so happy when he broke that run because that put us in control of the game. We ended up with two hundred eighty-nine yards rushing and then we got another interception return to put the game away. Eli only had to throw fifteen passes all game; I caught one ball and we were all just yelling in the locker room after the game, "We got in the tournament." Guys were pretty jacked 'cause now we were in the playoffs and you never know what can happen. It's single elimination, man.

But first we had to play New England at home. The 15–0 New England Patriots.

A Student of the Game

When I read *The GM* by Tom Callahan, the book about Ernie Accorsi, during the 2006 season, I saw that Eli Manning paid me a really nice compliment. Eli was talking about me as a player and said, "Plax is smarter than what you think, or what he shows you. In meetings, he doesn't say a lot. When he does say something, the coaches kind of look at him and wonder if he's taking it in or not. 'Is he half asleep?' 'Is he daydreaming?' But one time I couldn't find—this will sound bad—my playbook. So I grabbed Plax's book off the stool in front of his locker—our lockers are close by—to look up a formation or something. And when I opened it, I couldn't believe my eyes. He had written all of these notes in the margins—in beautiful handwriting. 'I'm the hot receiver here.' 'I go here.' 'I go there.' 'I do this or that.' 'Somebody else does whatever.' All in perfect penmanship. You know, it shouldn't have shocked me. If no one else knew Plaxico was in tune with the offense, I did. I knew how hard he worked. But I guess I didn't realize how committed he was to understanding exactly what he has to do on each play. It's almost like he doesn't want anybody to know he knows, but he does. As I say, you just can't see a player at a glance."

When I was in high school and college, I was just so much better than most everybody I played against that I didn't have to work on stuff. I would say, about the last year I was in Pittsburgh when I was with Coach Bruce Arians—my receivers coach then, and he's the offensive coordinator now—I started to learn about the little things. I felt like taking some notes. I started watching a lot more film. Then when I got to New York, I started taking little notes on what a guy's strengths were, what the cornerback does well, and what he doesn't do well, and it just kind of grew and evolved. When I was at Pittsburgh I just basically knew what I had to do. Now I understand what everybody does. I know all the calls and checks, I know all the signals. I know just about everything I can possibly know. It's to the point with me when I'm in the meetings and stuff, the coaches don't even ask me. They ask everybody else what they have to do. Like getting up on the board and drawing the plays. They don't even ask me because they know I know it.

What Coach Arians did was show me how the little things impact your game. The first time I came back to Pittsburgh for the minicamp after he was hired in 2004, I hadn't yet met him. He introduced himself and we had a six- or seven-minute conversation. Then he said, "Why don't you come upstairs to my office with me for a little bit?" I was thinking, *Oh, man, what does he want?* I didn't even know this guy, what did he want? So he sat me down and this was in May or June. He put on a tape, and I was thinking, *What the hell is wrong with this guy? He doesn't even know me.* So he told me all this shit I need to work on, right down to my steps as I start my pattern. He went, "You see this foot, you see the lead leg . . ." He showed me how when I started to run, my leg would first go backward before I started running. He explained that if I would eliminate that false step, this first step where I'm not going anywhere, that all these balls that are this close, just a few inches off, I would catch them.

As he was explaining it to me, I thought, Man, he's right. He's trying to help me out. I remember the first time I really watched film of myself. Then I would watch other guys like Carolina wide receivers Steve Smith and Isaac Bruce. I felt like those guys were doing the same thing as me in terms of running routes where we don't break down, we are just running in and out of cuts. Isaac and Torry Holt, they do it better than anybody. They don't break down, stop themselves to change direction. They're running in and out of cuts. So if I can learn to get rid of all these little problems at the line, I should be getting open like that more and more.

The bigger thing for me was that I had to learn this stuff. I had to know the whole offense if I was going to be the go-to guy. If I don't know what everybody else is doing, if I'm the number one receiver, the go-to guy, if I don't understand the concept with the offense and where everybody is at, then I can't be what I want to be. I just can't. As a number one receiver, I got guys asking me what they have all the time. Our rookie receiver Steve Smith (not the Carolina Steve Smith), everybody, they ask me, "What do I have on this play?" I say, "You got the curl," even if I'm on the other side of the formation. They don't want to ask Eli because they know if they ask Eli, he's not going to throw them the ball because they don't know what to do. So they ask me. "You got the hook, six yards." *Boom*, catch. You have to understand what people are doing around you so you can be even more successful. If Amani Toomer has a crossing route at twenty yards and I have a post, I know I have to get past the twenty-yard mark before I even break or I'm going to be running right into him. I got to run my guy off so he doesn't jump the crossing route and kill Amani.

I don't just know the routes, I know the depth for everything that everybody does. Once the coaches know that I know the whole offense, they can put me anywhere. It makes it harder to defend against me because I can play the Y position, I can play the Z, the X. They can put me on the inside slot, in the middle, on the outside, the strong side, or they can put me beside the tight end. I understand the whole concept of the offense. We were playing in London and I had an in-cut and Eli threw the ball behind me because running back Brandon Jacobs was in the wrong spot and pulled a defender into the spot where Eli was supposed to throw it. I said, "Brandon, you ran the wrong route."

He said, "What do you mean? I stay with the ball."

"No, you don't, you got the screen route. I got the end covered up."

On the sideline, we were still talking about it and I said, "Eli, tell Brandon he ran the wrong route." Eli said, "Yeah, man, you don't have the middle." Brandon thought about it and said, "Oh, my fault, man." That's cool, but my point is, I know what the backs do, I know what everybody does.

If I know what everybody is doing, that gives me more freedom to do what I want to do. I don't have to necessarily get to my route all the time if I know where this guy is going to break or where he's going to be.

That's why I say people really don't know me. They don't know what I study and the things that I look at and what I go through. It's like what Eli was saying about how people perceive me. My game is so down that I'm getting into the offensive line scheme. I'm asking Eli which way the line will slide on different protections. Why is the running back going back to the strong safety? That's where I'm trying to take my game to the next level. So now we all see these calls. If you get two to your side, if you're the second-man slot, you got to push out diagonally. Now I'm learning what the "fan" is, what a three-technique is. A fan is a blocking scheme against a certain rush. The offensive linemen just fan out and take their routes.

It's fun when you look at it like that. When I learn a route and I know that the time clock is going off and I've got to get to twelve yards but I can't because I got to push off a little bit and break it at nine, and I make the catch early, *boom.* Sometimes I sit down and we'll be watching a play, it will be maybe the third or fourth play they're showing us. We'll watch the defense we'll be playing against. It will be Wednesday or Thursday, and when everybody leaves, I'll be like, "Coach, I want you to look at this. Go back to the fourth play in that series when they are on the ten-yard line. You see them playing quarters coverage. Why can't we run this type of play? If they are going to play like this, why can't you put the Z on the crossing route and have me run the post behind him. If they are going to cut there like this, then I'm just going to be wide open. There's nobody there to cover me."

The coach will be like, "You're right, why don't you come over here on Tuesdays and help us put in plays." The coach may come back and say, "Hey, I ran it by, they said it's a good idea, but they've already got a game plan." That's okay, but I want them to know they can do different things and that I'm trying to come up with something. I don't just look at tape. I'll sit there and study it. I look at the linebackers. I see if I can read the linebacker based on if he's inside the defensive end or outside the defensive end, if he's giving any tips to what that secondary is going to be based on where he's lined up. If I can look at the weak-side linebacker and see every time that he jumps inside the defensive end it's a blitz or a free safety comes down to go under cover three, that gives me even more information. I'm two or three steps ahead of the ball game before the ball is even hiked, without even looking at the secondary. If somebody is deep on the end at the line of scrimmage or that real back is going to show me the coverage before the ball is hiked, then I just look at that guy.

See, the trick is not to look at the guys who are directly go-ing to cover you. They're going to try to trick you about what they're doing until they have to commit. A lot of the time, I don't even look at the safety on my side because there's noth-ing he's going to tell me. The safety can tell me nothing. I'm looking at a guy on the other side of him to figure it out. The guy on my side is going to play with me to try to disguise it. A lot of guys that play the X-receiver position, where I am more of the time, don't know that. They just go out and play. A lot of guys don't study the game enough to know that. There's only two or three coverages the defense can play, unless you got triple coverage or something. Pretty much, you're going to get a single, a bracket, or a double. There's only three things that you can possibly do. The faster you know it and you can pick up on it, the better. I tell Steve Smith and the other young guys on our team, "Hey, man, if you are thinking when you get to the line of scrimmage, you're already too late. If you are thinking when you are playing at this level, you're done. You're a step behind." When I get to the line, I just want to relax, I don't want to be thinking. I want to know my play calls, knowing what the defense is trying to do before the ball hikes.

My whole game is based on being fluid in and out of my cuts. I'm fast, but I'm not so blazing fast that I can just run away from the whole defense. That's why it was so important for me to learn all these little things a few years ago and then to take my game to the next level and start to understand the whole game. I'm a big guy and I know if I can get out of a break in three steps, then I'm that much harder to deal with. I was watching those other guys like Isaac Bruce. For them, they're so smooth that it's one, two, three, *boom*, and they're gone. That's why I try to run my routes like those guys. They are just so fluid and they're never breaking down and they're so crisp. Kind of like the route I ran in the Super Bowl. Don't break down, just run in and out of your cut. One, two, three, *boom*, get to the corner. You put the defensive back in a bad position as much as you can. Like with Ellis Hobbs on that play, I put him in a bad position and I didn't stop. If he was going to play way off and he was trying to take away the inside or the outside, I'd run hard at him and force him to make a decision. When I can run routes like that, defensive backs are scared of it. They fear it because you are not giving them anything to break on, nothing to read in your body language. You're just running and then, *boom*, you're gone.

I was able to do the same thing to Al Harris in the NFC Championship Game.

One time I ran a cut and I took an inside release. I just stopped on a dime and came back and snatched the ball out of the air. The defense can't cover me when I'm running routes like that. It's almost impossible. My game is deception. I always try to do the exact opposite of what the defense is trying to not let me do. That will frustrate guys all the time. If a guy is taking away your inside and you can still beat him inside, it's like, "Whoa, your coach is going to get you. You know you're not supposed to let me inside." That freaks those guys out. You can really screw a guy's day up like that. That really gets them fired up.

The thing for me is that I really try to appreciate what the coaches are telling me about the game. It took a while for me to get it because when I was young, I didn't have to do all this stuff to be great. I was just better than other people. But I look back on it and think about it. It's like this letter I sent to Ken Mannie, the Michigan State strength-and-conditioning coach. He was nice enough to put it in a magazine article he wrote in 2007.

I wrote:

Dear Coach Mannie:

First off, I hope that you and your beautiful family are doing well. Over ten years have passed since I first stepped
onto MSU's campus, and I wish I knew then what I know
now. Maybe I wouldn't have been so hardheaded. But
thanks to you for always pushing me, even though I
thought I knew it all. You will always be one of my favorite
people because you always told the truth and never sugar-
coated anything.

Mannie told *USA Today* in an article before the Super Bowl:
"I think the letter he wrote, which is in my scrapbook, says it all
about how much he has grown up . . . Would he have been able
to write that letter 10 years ago? Probably not. But the fact that
he can now makes me really proud . . . His maturity, or lack of
it, has led to his struggles at times, but no one can say he's a bad
person."

15

New England and Beyond

We were getting ready to play New England on Saturday night—the last game of the regular season. The hype was huge—we found out that the game wasn't just going to be on NFL Network but on both CBS and NBC, because the league couldn't work it out with the cable companies, and the government wasn't too happy.

Although we were already in the playoffs, I was playing. It's a whole week, including practice and the game. I was coming around and I was starting to feel better as the week went on. I told Coach Coughlin, "Coach, I'm going to practice this week." He was like, "Huh? You feeling better?" I said, "Yeah, I'm starting to feel like I can get a few reps." I went out and practiced a few plays, got some reps, and I started making moves and started jumping. The coaches were getting scared, so they told me, "That's enough." They didn't want me to aggravate anything. I was just healing up. But the ankle was feeling better and everybody could see it. I was starting to feel wonderful. Then, after the Buffalo game, I said, "I'm back, I'm ready."

There were a lot of people in the media talking about whether we should rest the starters or play them. We just approached it like another game, really. My whole thing was, I wanted to play this game because I was starting to hit my stride. The other thing was that I was the only person on the team who had ever beaten those guys up to that point. I wanted to play because they are bullies. They are arrogant, they're cocky, and they just want to come into your house and talk trash to you. I played against them several times and this was how they were. I told the guys coming into it that it was going to be physical. They were going to be taking cheap shots, hitting you after the whistle. This is how they are, they just want to get you off your game. People say the Patriots are classy? Classy, my ass. What is the definition of *classy* here? When they go to work on Sundays, the whole damn team talks trash, even Mike Vrabel.

It's funny. I played with Mike in Pittsburgh and he was quiet as a church mouse. He went to New England and he wanted to talk trash with the rest of the team. I was like, "Vrabel, come on, let's be friends here. Let's be real. This is not who you are. You're not a talker. Come on, Vrabel, be out with yourself." He didn't say nothing, just looked at me and we laughed. "Come on, Vrabel, you're talking trash?" But their biggest trash talker is Rodney Harrison, without question. And he's a cheap-shot artist. An absolute artist. If you were blocking him and you get the best of him, after the play he'll keep pushing. But during the play, he'll be, "Oh, oh, oh, the ball went the other way." He wants you to chill out and not touch him, but the next damn play he is looking for your ass. Cheap shots. If he can't get the best of you, he's going to butter you up, make you think he's cool. He's one of them. As soon as you relax, he's going to try to knock you into next week. That's Rodney—trashy.

He's a good player. Smart, physical. I like Rodney; he's cool with me. But we have run-ins all the time on that football field. I'm ready, I ain't backing down. He can take cheap shots with me all he wants, but he better go find somebody else to pick on.

He'll say, "Oh, you ain't going to do shit. What you gonna do? You ain't going to do nothing." I'll say, "All right, we'll see." And then as soon as I go try to block him, he'll go, "Hey, why are you trying to hurt me?" I go, "Man, I'm doing my job, you do yours. Stop crying." He's a funny guy.

The other guy who talks on their team is Vince Wilfork. Nonstop, oh my God. Big-time trash talker. Tedy Bruschi don't talk at all. He's cool. But he's one of those guys who looks weird when he plays. His feet flap in the air all the time and you think, *Man, how is this guy making plays? How is he making interceptions?* He is so unorthodox and so awkward. I would say if Tedy played anywhere else but in New England, he wouldn't be a middle linebacker. The coaches would look at him and he'd look so unathletic. But he's been playing for years and getting the job done. What can you say? Nothing.

I wanted to go out and make some routes full speed and make some plays. Once we got on that field, man, the game was so physical and so fast. We never thought about losing the game. That was our mind-set. Our mind-set was they were coming to our house trying to get the undefeated record. Hey, not on my watch, not going to happen. They were not going to do it here. That was our whole thing, that they wouldn't make history here; we were going to make history.

Yeah, so they made history. Give them a lot of credit. Those guys do a great job. Belichick is just awesome at scouting the other team. They don't bring a lot of superstars at you, but he puts them in a position to do well, and those guys seem to like playing for Belichick because they know they got a chance to win. They get guys to fit in and the guys know what they're getting into.

As soon as we got back in the locker room after the game, Coach Coughlin said, "Hey, we got to worry about Tampa Bay. See y'all on Wednesday. Peace." Nobody was really mad or upset.

We checked ourselves, and if they say they are the best team in the world and they just get by us, we figured if we go out and play the way we just played for the next three or four weeks, maybe we'll get to play them again.

The thing about that game was we came away feeling really confident that if we got them again, we'd have a chance. We had a 28–16 lead on them in the second half. Yeah, they scored two touchdowns and got up 31–28, but then we give up an interception with ten minutes left when Eli was throwing down the sideline for me. They got the ball at midfield and scored. If we got rid of that mistake, I think the game would turn out differently. Our defense gave up some points, but we stopped them early and kept them to field goals on three of their four scoring drives in the first half. Plus, we weren't really giving them a big pass rush. I had four catches for eighty-four yards and two touchdowns. I also had a fifty-two-yard reception on the first drive, so it wasn't like they just dominated us or anything. They won the game, but we were right there with them and we didn't feel like we even gave them our best shot.

Aside from the Patriots going undefeated in the regular season, both Tom Brady (fifty touchdowns) and Randy Moss (twenty-three touchdown catches) got their records. That stuff didn't mean much other than they beat us. I'm a big Moss fan and Brady is obviously Brady, can't take anything away from him. But the interesting thing for me to watch was how they used wide receiver Wes Welker. He had eleven catches for 122 yards against us in that game and he caught something like 112 for the season. I knew he was quick; I've seen him return a few kicks and punts. But whoa, that offense they got over there, especially with Brady running it. Man, Welker can do whatever he wants. I think it got to a point in the season where they weren't even running routes.

They were just running where the people weren't. It was very obvious. They will put Welker on a play, on a read. I guarantee they called the Z-option or Z-read, and he and Tom just read it. If the defense runs one-on-one coverage, Welker has the option to go inside, outside, hook it up. If the cornerback sits down on the route, Welker just runs through. If you look at their tapes, nobody gets open that much. You just don't, not if you just call a play. If you just call a pass play in the offense and the guy is open that much, there's no way. There's no way that the defenses he plays against are that out of position every week. It's just not humanly possible. A coach is not that smart. There's no way that you know where the guys aren't going to be every time you go to this guy, the guy catching that many balls, catching ten, eleven balls a game. They're giving him the option to run away from the coverage. It's really impressive to see what he does with it and how him and Brady are on the same page so much.

There's no way to defend that unless you just put two guys on him the whole time. The week we played Atlanta on a Monday-night game, I was out to dinner with Byron Leftwich. We were at Morton's Steakhouse and we were sitting there watching the Patriots-Dallas game on Sunday night. They had Moss on the outside and they got Wes in the slot. Wes does have a half-peel motion, goes to the center and turns around and goes out. I guess Dallas had watched so much of him running a little hook route that the linebacker shifted over to take away the inside break and safety Ken Hamlin comes down to take away the outside break. So when the ball was hiked, Wes just ran through to the wide-open space past Hamlin. That's how you know that the offense is running an option route. There's no way that you make that play call in the huddle for that defense. With Brady being the quarterback, Wes is unstoppable. Wes is always going to find the open spot and he's going to get there so quick. He's not fast, but he gets open so quick. It's sharp, man. Wes makes a move and *boom*, he's open and Brady has it there for him.

I wouldn't say that the New England game was a turning point, but we felt pretty good about ourselves after that game going into Tampa Bay. To me, it showed we could play with them. I've played New England six times since they started winning Super Bowls and now I'm 3–3 against them. I was 2–2 with Pittsburgh and then the Giants played them twice last season. There's no question that they're the toughest team in the league as far as adjustments, all the things they can throw at you. Whenever you play them, it seems like they got fourteen or fifteen guys on the field, not just eleven. That's how good their scheme is. What they force you to do is nickel-and-dime them all the time. They're not going to let you do what you do best and they're not going to make mistakes. What you gotta do is don't make mistakes, either. That's what we talked about all week going into the Super Bowl. Don't make mistakes, don't let them capitalize on them.

We didn't have too much time to think about it because we were going right back in the next day to watch a little bit of Tampa Bay tape. We came in Sunday morning and we were there for an hour. So we really didn't even have a chance to think about the Patriots because we were right back in the next day watching a tape of Tampa Bay, a team we don't know at all.

We played Tampa Bay in 2006 and that was the tape we looked at Sunday, the one when they came to Giants Stadium. We came out saying that they were going to try to stop our running game. That's basically what they did. They were out there playing one-on-one on the corners. Hey, man, if they wanted to go out there and play us one-on-one, that's just damn disrespect for us. It's kind of along the lines of what Tampa Bay cornerback Ronde Barber said that week. He was quoted in the *New York Post* saying, "Plax is kind of a special athlete. Not that he's overly fast or real, like Randy Moss, athletic, because that's not his game. But he's a bitch to deal with." So I get a copy of that and highlight all of it except the last sentence. I tell everyone, Randy Moss is the best wide receiver in the league. But you start start saying I'm not athletic? *Damn*. That got me fired up. Like I said that week, "They got the best defense in the league; they should be riding high and not worrying about us."

One thing I'll say is we were pretty loose, ready for that game at Tampa Bay. I got Steve Smith, our rookie wide receiver, pretty good the Friday before the game, when we were getting ready to go down there. For each position, the rookies have to get breakfast on the travel days or any other days we don't get breakfast brought in by the team. Steve was supposed to be getting the breakfast. So the first time in training camp, Steve forgot and he said, "I was running late." I said, "All right, don't let it happen again." So he did it again and the vets started getting on me, saying, "Come on, you got to do something." I said all right, but I let it go, gave him a chance. Later on in training camp, Steve rode back up the hill in Albany with me on the cart. Normally only vets ride the carts up to the locker room. Osi Umenyiora saw that and was like, "No, man, don't tell me you're getting soft, you let the rookie ride the cart with you, too?" Then the third time he forgot breakfast, I said, "Steve, why didn't you get no breakfast?" He said, "I ain't going to get no damn breakfast." I was like, "Okay, that's cool."

Friday, we were getting ready to leave to go to Tampa for the playoffs. He was supposed to get breakfast for the Tampa game. He had a brand-new dress shirt in the bag folded up. I took the shirt out of the bag and cut the sleeves off and folded it up and put it back in the plastic. Then I took his socks and put that dye that the FBI uses for tracing money in them and took one of his dress shoes. The shoes that he had were sweet, brand-new dress shoes that still had the tag on them; they were $295.

Everybody was getting ready to get on the bus, right? Steve was in the locker room getting ready to put on his shirt. He opened it up out of the plastic and he looks at it, thought about it, and puts it on and the arms pop out. The whole team busted out laughing. I said, "The next time I tell you you better have something, you better have my sandwich." Then Brandon London was supposed to bring the sandwiches and one Saturday he didn't bring them. I took all his clothes and put them in the shower on the floor. He had nothing—he had to wear the New York Giants sweats home. They were nice clothes, too. Nice shirt, shoes, very nice. I said, "Next time y'all forget, I'm going to take your car keys, and then I'm going to take your girlfriend." After that, we'd be getting IHOP. The rookies stepped it up. Whatever we wanted. We were eating real good.

We got to Tampa for the game and they had a drive to go up 7–0. We went three-and-out the first three times we got the ball. I went to Gilbride and was like, "Coach, they are out there playing us one-on-one. Why are we trying to run the ball with an eight-, nine-man front?" In those first three drives, we threw once on first down, but it was a three-yard pass to tight end Kevin Boss. We needed to get it outside to either me or Amani. So then we opened up. Eli got a short one to me, then he hit Amani three straight times for seventeen, ten, and thirteen yards. Then we set up this nice screen to Brandon Jacobs for the touchdown. It was sweet and now it was 7–7.

Our defense got Tampa to go three-and-out and we get the ball back right away. We put Ahmad Bradshaw out there. He was our little rookie running back we got out of Marshall in the seventh round. Ahmad Bradshaw, oh man, you're talking about tough. He runs with no conscience. In that Tampa Bay game, he was itching to get in, and then he got in and he just took the game over. The first play of this drive, we put him in and he met Derrick Brooks, the All-Pro, Defensive Player of the Year linebacker, in the hole and he ran slap over Derrick Brooks for eight yards. I was like, "Oooh, you just got ran over," talking to Derrick Brooks because Ahmad was running so hard. Brooks was hitting him, but Ahmad was like, *boom.* He was running through linebackers and they couldn't bring him down. He changed that whole game around for us. And then the coaches had no choice but to play him.

Then Eli hit me for eleven and nine yards, he got Steve Smith for twenty-one yards, Bradshaw for nine, and now we had Tampa Bay totally backpedaling. They were trying to run all these delay coverages at Eli, where the linebackers were hesitating before they jumped into the throwing lanes, but Eli saw it all. He was playing really sharp in this game. He went twenty for twenty-seven, only 185 yards and two touchdowns, but he was so smart. Never forced anything and read all the coverages. Jacobs ran in the last eight yards for the touchdown and we were up 14–7. From there, our defense just dominated the rest of the way, intercepted Jeff Garcia twice, and came up with a fumble on the opening kickoff of the second half. Amani came up with a nice four-yard touchdown catch in the fourth quarter to put us up 24–7. The Bucs got a touchdown, but it was over.

So it was back to Dallas. Now, the whole thing about Tony Romo going to Cabo San Lucas or wherever he went, that was so ridiculous to me. It was a bye week, so he was supposed to be as far away from football as he possibly could get. Guys like me do it all the time. Guys do it during the regular season—go to Cabo, the Bahamas, wherever you can go to just get away from football for a few days. It was only because he was with Jessica Simpson that he got noticed. You think if he and Jason Whitten went out there on their own the press would have made such a big deal out of it? Come on, man, it was because of who he was with that it got so many headlines. The guy has been doing it for years, man, going on vacation on a bye week, just trying to get away from it. We were trying to concentrate on winning the football game, not reading into the hype that he wasn't focused and all that.

Romo going on vacation wasn't some insult or anything. Dallas beat us twice and we didn't want to get swept. We didn't want to lose to those guys three times and we knew that it was going to be the hardest game we were going to play up to that point. Everybody knew about their offense and how special they are, and their defense and how good they are. We weren't really thinking about that. We were just thinking about winning the game. What ticked us off a little bit was when we were watching the Green Bay–Seattle game the day before. The Packers won and we hadn't even played yet, it was Saturday. Brett Favre got on TV and said, "Yeah, I can't wait to go to Dallas next week." We sat up. "Are you serious? We haven't even played the game yet!" So Brett Favre already knew he was going to Dallas. He wanted revenge on those guys from when he had gone down there and Dallas whupped up on them. Brett Favre didn't have any respect for us. It was the topic of discussion in our meeting that night.

Coughlin brought it up right away. He said, "Hell, people don't have any respect for us. Brett Favre got on TV and says he's going to Dallas next week? Oh, hell, no, not on my watch." That just shows you how much players around the league had respect for us. We were a joke to them. I have a lot of respect for Brett Favre. I think he's the best quarterback who ever played, the best to ever put a uniform on. For him to say that to us, it was just disrespectful. We didn't like that at all. When we had a chance to play those guys, you couldn't have written the story any better.

The Dallas game was pretty tight in the first half. They went up 14–7 with a minute left in the first half. From the last part of the first quarter, they'd been rolling. They had a ninety-six-yard drive to tie it and then they went ahead on this twenty-play, ninety-yard drive. They took more than ten minutes off the clock. Just a long-ass drive and we were just sitting there for what felt like forever. Then our two-minute offense did it again. Actually, it was a one-minute offense in this situation. When we get in the two-minute mode, our antennae just go up a little bit higher. We know how to get it done in that situation. We'd been very successful in that ever since I'd been in New York. I don't know that there was any particular reason for it. Eli just buckled down and he made all the calls. He was making all the calls at the line of scrimmage, giving out signals, and we were just running off him.

I think Dallas thought we were going to play kind of conservatively, maybe just go for a field goal. Eli hit Steve Smith for a couple of nice gains of twenty-two and eleven yards. Then Dallas made a big mistake and got called for a face-mask penalty on Smith's second catch. In no time we're in their territory with two time-outs left. We're going for a score. Eli tried to hit me in the end zone, but it was incomplete. We got to third-and-ten and he hit Boss for nineteen yards. Then he hit Amani for the touchdown and all that momentum the Cowboys had on those two long drives was gone.

Steve Smith was huge in the playoffs. Every game, he had some big catch. He had that twenty-one-yarder against Tampa Bay on our second touchdown drive and took it right up to the end of the Super Bowl when he had a big third-down catch before Eli threw me the game-winning touchdown. I called him the secret weapon. With his intangibles at wide receiver, he was made to play this game. He was crafty, he was fast enough, but his separation was just unbelievable. I tell guys if they can beat man-to-man coverage at this level and separate from a defender, they can play forever. Steve's feet never stop moving. He's got that little quick, one-two boom. I taught him all my best moves—flip a little elbow in a tight press coverage to get a man off you, maybe pull on the guy's jersey a little bit to get leverage—and he picked it up right away.

He took it all in, and he put it into his game. He didn't play like a rookie, he just did it. Some of the plays that he's made in big games and crunch time, his mind never wavers. He never thought about how big the stage he was on was, he just focused on catching the football and getting open. We got to the point that we had plays in just for him. Against Dallas's third-best defensive back, he would beat that guy every time.

Now, Steve is a little goofy. A little ding-y. His common sense—uh, wait, he doesn't have good common sense. Like in meetings, the coach tells him something—it will be a big game like Dallas—then, fifteen minutes later, the coach will ask Steve about it and Steve will say, "What are you talking about?" Oh man, come on, Steve. Gilbride would be like, "This is serious, this is serious. If this guy blitzes, you have to break hot." Steve says, "Oh, okay, I got you, I got you." Then we'd get to the walk-through practice. The defense would run the blitz and Steve would just run his route and everybody would be like, "Come on, Steve, get it together, man. You sat through the meeting and he told you twice." Once again, "Oh, okay, I'll get it next time." Very California. He gets it, but you gotta tell him over and over and over. You gotta beat him over the head. But once he gets it, he'll never forget it. His attention span is not real good in a meeting, but he's a smart player.

He's not a real big chalkboard guy. He's not a classroom guy. We have to worry about it; we quiz him and ask him and keep going over and over. If you don't, he'll blow it. But he gets the job done and we love playing with him.

I gotta say, this is the best group of receivers I've ever played with. Take Amani Toomer—I wouldn't want to play beside anybody else. He's a terrific person and a crafty receiver with great hands, and he brings something special to our offense. He's a jokester, always having a good time, but he's a pro. I'm talking about the leading receiver in New York Giants history. That's not something small.

In the Green Bay game, he caught a couple of balls and he was saying, "Come on, Plax, we need more. We need more from you. You gotta go, let's go." I was like, "All right, man, sit down. It's cold." He was in my face: "Get up, man. Come on, we need some more. You gotta do more." I'm like, "All right, man." We all celebrate one another's success, pumping one another up. I think that's special. Especially when you got a guy like me coming in, and basically I took his position, the X, and he moved over to the Z. I have a lot of respect for that guy. He works hard and plays hard. This is his thirteenth season coming up.

In 2006, I didn't know how much I missed him until he went down. I was getting so much double and triple coverage. Without him around to keep the defense honest and take advantage of stuff like that, it was hard. Real hard. It impacted everybody. For Eli, Toom was his safety blanket. Toom is very dependable. He's probably been our most consistent player for the past couple of years when he's in catching the balls, running the routes, and just being where he's supposed to be, while sometimes I make up my own shit.

Funny thing about Toom is he's real forgetful. He'll go the wrong way coming out of the huddle at least five or six times a game. He'll come over to the left and I look at him and say, "You're on the right side, dude?" He knows the play, it's just that he played X for so long, like ten years, and then I got there and the coaches moved him to the Z. He would come out of the huddle and go the wrong way, and I'd say, "Toom," and the coaches would say, "Come on, Amani, help us out." It's a joke now. He does it so much that the coaches ask me, "Plaxico, honestly, how many times have you put Toom in the right position?" At least five or six times a game. Sometimes we'd be at the line of scrimmage and he'll ask me, "What's the play?" I'll say, "Level, level, level." Then he'll say, "What do I got?" I'll say, "The under," just as Eli says, "Hike." Yes, that's Toom.

To everybody else, it looks like we know what's going on within the plays, but Toom, he's lost until I tell him exactly what to do. He'll be like, "Thanks, man, thanks." This was a funny one. We were playing Atlanta on a Monday night, so we were in a two-minute mode and right beside each other. I went up to the line and said, "What's the play?" He said, "Level, level." "Hike." So I ran the level and I know as soon as I took off, I knew it was the wrong play. He told me the wrong play. I come off to the sidelines and I said, "Toom, you told me the wrong play, man." He said, "I did? My bad, man, my bad. I didn't mean to do it. Hey, you should have known what the play was yourself." I said, "Okay, okay, I'm going to see what happens the next time you ask me what the play is. I'm going to give you the wrong route." We were like on the five-yard line. He caught the ball on the three-yard line, and if I was right behind him, he probably would have scored. Instead, he got stopped and we got a field goal. I got to the sidelines and Coach Sullivan said, "What happened?"

I said, "Coach, I don't even want to tell you."

"What you mean?"

I said, "Toom told me the wrong play."

Sullivan said, "Why did you ask Toom?"

"Because I didn't get the signal, I didn't get the call."

Sullivan said, "You had the nerve to ask Toom?"

One day in practice, Amani ran the wrong route six or seven times. We were like, "Toom, what's wrong with you today?" He said, "Man, I'm just in a funk." "Five or six times you're in a funk?" "I know, man, I know. My mind is not with me today."

Back to the Dallas game. It was 14–14 at halftime. Dallas came out and got a field goal on the first drive of the second half. We traded a couple of possessions, but then our punt returner, R. W. McQuarters, got a nice 25-yard return to put us at the Dallas 37-yard line with a minute left in the third quarter. Now it was Eli's turn again to keep doing what he's been doing for weeks now, just peppering them with passes. He hit Amani for 13 yards, Boss for 4, Smith for 4, and then Smith again for 11. We were at the Dallas 9-yard line just like that. That was just how Eli did it in the playoffs, efficient, no mistakes, big plays when he had to. He was twelve of eighteen for 163 yards and two touchdowns in this game. Not big numbers, but he played so big.

We ran it in from there with Brandon Jacobs getting the touchdown to make it 21–17. From there, our defensive guys just played physical up front. Dallas has some big boys out there: Leonard Davis, Marco Columbo. I've never seen a team like that. They got some big dudes out there, man. Damn. That just showed you that our defense was relentless that game. They just hit the switch and started killing people.

In the playoffs, middle linebacker Antonio Pierce would get the whole defense together, and they would watch films as a unit without coaches being there. They would do that for maybe an hour and a half or two hours after practice during the whole playoffs. I knew they were focused and it showed, too. Antonio is the dude for the defense. He's the one who puts all the guys in position. He's the one who makes all the calls. They really took the defensive scheme to the next level. They had an understanding of when Antonio made a call—when he said, "I'm going to help over here on the wing, so if I make this call, you cannot let him get behind you"—they were doing some things that were a little unorthodox. They knew what was going on from front to back, and it showed. Antonio just didn't want to lose. If he lost, he'd be dogging himself. He drove them every day, by themselves, with no coaches in there Wednesday through Friday.

The other guy who was big in all of that was Michael Strahan. He was such a big factor, whether he was making the play himself or if he was creating something for the other guys up front. Our front guys, Stray, Osi, and Justin Tuck, were just huge in the playoffs. For Stray, that's the last thing he needed to solidify his career; this was the icing on the cake for him. With all the things he went through the last couple of years, like getting divorced and having his ex-wife say all sorts of stuff and having to fight her in court, he never lost his cool. He never let anybody see him sweat even if he was hurting inside. I never saw it, nobody else ever saw it. He dealt with it by himself or through his parents or whoever. He never complained one time. He never talked about it to anybody in public. He kept everything that was going on in his personal life to himself. He never brought it up, he handled it the right way. It was like it never happened. During the season nobody ever talked about it. Now he's happier than I've ever seen him. He's ecstatic, got a new girlfriend, and is traveling. He's a world champion. I don't know if he's going to retire or not. We haven't talked about that. He's having so much fun right now. He can still play, no question about that. It's just about whether he wants to do it or not, it's totally up to him. Me, I wouldn't expect him to come back, but knowing the kind of person that he is, he'll probably return.

In this Dallas game, our defense got in there and hit Romo and got him frustrated. It really showed on those last three drives. Right after the touchdown, they sacked Romo to put Dallas in third-and-thirteen on that drive. We stopped them. The next drive, Romo was called for intentional grounding after they got to our forty-one-yard line. Huge play that killed that drive. Then McQuarters ended the final drive by intercepting Romo on the last play. Our defense was just huge against them, especially after they scored a lot on us during the regular season. Can't say enough about our defense.

Now it was on to Green Bay to freeze our asses off. Brett Favre wasn't expecting us.

16

Freezing in Green Bay

Everybody remembers how red Tom Coughlin's face was during the NFC Championship Game at Green Bay. Everybody knows it was minus one degree (that's minus twenty-three with the windchill factor). Amani Toomer said after that game that if you had any quit in you as a person, those conditions would make you quit. I agree with that. Let me say this, if that game wasn't for us to get into the Super Bowl, I don't think I would have played. I'm serious. That was ridiculous. I probably would have said, "Man, my calf or something hurts. I don't know what it is, but something don't feel right." When you tried to spit, the spit would freeze to the face mask of your helmet.

But I'll also say this: That day we woke up and we ate and got on the bus, I'd never seen my teammates look like that. I don't think anybody said a thing the whole ride. The ride was at least forty minutes long. Nobody said a word. My boys were ready, I know we were ready. I could just tell. Everybody was just looking out the window and taking it all in. There was nothing but country land on that highway. Even after the ride, when we were in the locker room, guys knew what we had at stake. For me, this was the third time I'd been to a conference championship game and I was like, "Man, we just got to get to the doorstep, I'm not going home again."

That weather, man, I can't even explain how bad it was. I didn't know it could get that cold. I ran outside with my tights on, I put a little long-sleeve shirt on and I ran outside and I ran like three or four routes and said to Eli, "E, I got to go." I said, "I can't feel my fingers." It was gone, it was like somebody had pumped air into my gloves and I couldn't feel them. I said, "Oh shit, man, I'm going to have a problem." It was too fucking cold. What was I going to do? I wasn't out there ten minutes and I couldn't feel my hands. What was I going to do? I never wore tights before, skintights. So I came in, "Yo, man, whatever y'all got, I need it." So I got lubed down in Vaseline from neck to feet, and I put the tights on.

We had these feet warmers. They're supposed to attach to your socks or you put them in your shoes and then you wear them. I was like, "Fuck that, man." I got some athletic tape and taped them to the bottom of my feet. Not on top of my insole or to my shoes. I taped it to my feet—to the bare skin. Head trainer Ronnie Barnes was like, "Plaxico, you can't do that. Your feet are going to be on fire." I said, "That's what I need. Do you know how cold it is out there?" I said, "Shit, let 'em burn. I'm not going to freeze." So my feet are really hot because those warmers do get hot. I'm running late, the guys are already out there on the sideline. Then I put my turtleneck on, and I put a sleeveless tight suit on top of that. You know them skully hats we have, like ski hats? I cut that in half with scissors and put that over my neck. That was that black thing that I had on my neck.

I don't like wearing nothing under my helmet, but I had every inch of skin aside from my face covered. I had that skully hat and a big-ass turtleneck. You can look at the pictures, it's so funny. It's like guys were asking, "What is that you got on?" I said, "This is my face warmer." The other thing the equipment guys did that week is they had some guy come in and he put sheep fleece on the inside of our helmets. It was perfect for the helmets. They were like sticky on one side so they wouldn't move around. We had helmet fur. I guess it worked a little bit. You could feel a little difference on your ears.

It was just anything you could do to get even the slightest bit warmer and we pulled out every trick. Anything; psychologically, we needed it. We didn't have Gatorade on the sideline. It was all chicken broth. No water, no Gatorade, just chicken broth. I don't remember drinking any water until halftime or maybe after the game.

The other thing is that our equipment director, Joe Skiba, and some of the other equipment guys went to a ski shop, like a Ski Barn or something, and they got these huge-ass mittens. They have a thumb on them and they come way up your arms, like all the way to your elbows. So we had three pair of those and we put like ten of those warmers in the gloves, too. So I was on the sidelines and keeping my hands warm. Then they gave me this coat that covered me all the way down over my knees and that trapped the heat coming off the ground from the heaters. Those mittens, they had to be like eighty or ninety degrees, it was unbelievable. They saved me. It was so cold. When I started catching the ball so good, everybody was like, "How were you catching the ball like that?" I said, "I don't know how, I was out there just doing it." But they had those mittens and they saved me. I learned during that 2004 AFC Championship Game against New England not to act all brave. I had gone out in my regular uniform, but that game was so cold that I couldn't really function. I didn't wear any heavy stuff and I was frozen by the end.

Some of the guys came out with just the shirtsleeves on. The offensive linemen were talking about doing that all week. I'm telling you, that's stupid. I don't care where you from or where you grow up, when it's minus twenty-three with the windchill, you're cold. There's no mental thing. There's no, "I'm a tough guy." You're just cold. I don't believe in none of that Green Bay mystique or any of the Lambeau Field stuff. You can't get used to that. It's not human for you to be used to that.

We did every trick, every little thing we could think of. I sat on that sideline and kept my hands in those mittens as long as I could, and when I had to go out there, I sprinted out there. Every play, my hands went in that little hand roll on my uniform, and I just caught balls as best I could. Right before every play, as they were about to hike the ball, I pulled them out, ran my route, and caught the ball. Then my hands went right back into the hand warmers. The good thing about the field there in Green Bay is that it has heaters under the ground, so the field didn't get frozen and hard. It was pretty soft. But if you got hit by another guy, damn, that hurt. If you took a helmet to the thigh or shoulder, that was tough. That was the most painful game I ever played in. It was three and a half hours of pain for one of the best feelings of my life. But I'll tell you, getting hit by another guy—brutal. I was wondering what Charles Woodson was thinking about when he got run over on that first play by Brandon Jacobs. I think Brandon knocked Woodson silly.

The other thing we did was during TV time-outs, we went to the sideline and got next to the heaters. I talked to Fred Taylor before the game and he said, "Hey, man, look, I'm going to tell you this is a real veteran move right here. On them TV time-outs, don't be standing outside on that field, be over there by that heater until the referee gives you a twenty-second call. Then it's time to go back on the field." So on every TV time-out we had, I was on the sidelines by the heater. All of the receivers did that. I was like, "Come on and stand by this heater. Hey, ref, give me a twenty-second call." At twenty seconds, you get the call and go. Then Packers cornerback Al Harris and the other guys from Green Bay noticed and they started doing it. But we had a little advantage for a while.

I'll say this, with doing all that stuff, making sure we did everything we could, I felt pretty good. My hands felt warm the whole game and that's why I had the game I had. I caught eleven balls for 154 yards and I forced Al Harris into an illegal-contact penalty that wiped out an interception he got. People thought it was amazing and I was just all over him all game.

The whole thing with me getting hurt against Harris in the second game of the season, there was no wanting revenge for that. He wasn't trying to hurt me. It's just football. He's a Pro Bowler and he gave me a lot of respect. He came out and said he thought I'm one of the top five receivers in the game. That was enough for me. I didn't have to dog him or anything like that, but we were going at it during the NFC Championship Game. We were talking a lot of shit to each other during the game. That was just competitors going at it and the Super Bowl was the next game. We all wanted to get there. After the game, he said again that I'm one of the top five receivers in the league. There was no need for me to talk, there was nothing else for me to say. Now, Deion Sanders on NFL Network, that was different. Deion was like, "Al Harris is the best corner in the league, he's a shutdown corner. To be honest with you, Plaxico Burress can't beat him." When I saw Deion for an NFL Network interview during Super Bowl week, I got up there and the first thing I said was, "First of all, you said Al Harris would shut me down." Deion said, "Yeah, I didn't think you were going to do that to him." I said, "All right, I just wanted to let you know I heard that."

Just playing against a player like Harris was enough to get me going. It's like I said that week before the game, "He's a Pro Bowl corner and they say when you get voted to the Pro Bowl, you're one of the elite guys in the league. They're going to come out and play us the way we know they're going to come out and play us, so it's going to come down to me and him." I knew I was going to get one-on-one coverage against him because that's what Green Bay did the first time and that's what they always do. They had Harris on one side and Charles Woodson on the other. Those guys are serious veterans, good players, so the Packers depend on them two to get it done. But when I get to play like that, I humiliate a whole lot of guys. The guys that come out and say we're just going to cover you with one guy—I love it. There is nothing better than a man-on-man challenge.

What I knew is I had to attack Harris and get him out of his game right away. He wants to be physical, tie you up at the line of scrimmage as much as he can. I knew I was going to have to fight him off. I had studied a lot of tape of Harris during the week. I said after the game, "I knew if I could get away from the line of scrimmage, get his hands off me, I could make some plays. It was a physical battle, but I won that battle." We also knew he didn't track the ball very well. What Harris does is pay so much attention to the receiver that he doesn't look back for the ball. So we hit a lot of quick stuff against him. Run right at him, turn and *boom*. Eli was right on with those passes all game.

The first drive was key for a lot of what we did as the game went on. The Packers were loading up trying to stop the run, and Eli hit a bunch of quick passes. He hit me for six, nineteen, and eleven yards. All of them went for first downs, including one on third-and-ten to keep the drive going. We got a field goal and a 3–0 lead right away. We came back in the second quarter and he hit me twice more for seven and eighteen yards on the way to another field goal. It was 6–0, but we had the confidence to believe we could move it on these guys. Green Bay got the lead before halftime with kind of a fluke touchdown to Donald Driver and then a field goal, but we were feeling real confident.

The one really bad thing before halftime is that Green Bay safety Atari Bigby came up and nailed me on the shoulder, separated my shoulder. I didn't think it was that bad at first, but then I had to go down to get a pass late in the first half. I fell on the shoulder and it hurt like hell and I dropped the ball. With about twenty seconds left in the first half, I got to the locker room and took a shot to make sure that it was okay. Had to do the same thing for the Super Bowl.

We came out in the second half and drove right down on them. Eli hit me on a second-and-eight for nine yards and a first down. Then it's third-and-nine and Harris got the illegal contact when he pushed me out of the way to get the interception. Really obvious call. I think he was getting frustrated. Then we got another second-and-seven and Eli hit me for eighteen to get us to the Green Bay eleven-yard line. Brandon Jacobs then took it the rest of the way, scoring a touchdown to give us a 13–10 lead. That drive was key 'cause we ran the ball so much, nine times, that I think we really started to get Green Bay out of their game. They had four penalties on that drive. The one with Harris on me, then a roughing penalty that wiped out an incomplete pass on a third-and-five, and then two more offside calls on their defensive tackles, including that big trash talker Cullen Jenkins. That dude just never stops. I mean, lots of guys talk trash, but usually they just do it a little and then they stop and just play. That dude, it's constant. He's yelling, "You can't run the ball over here." He'll make like one play and say, "I told you, I told you." It's like, "Man, will you just shut the fuck up so we can just play football and get on out of here."

Green Bay came back and got the lead, but then we responded right away. We were facing second-and-ten at the Green Bay thirty-five-yard line and Eli hit Toomer with a huge play for twenty-three yards right on the sideline. This is where Amani

Toomer is at his best. He's always inbounds on the sideline. We call it Classic Toom. You see some of the catches that he makes dragging his feet? What about the one in Seattle two years ago? Sick. The ball was up in the air and he did a three-sixty, caught the ball over his head, and before he went out, he tapped his heel inbounds. That was so sweet and is so smooth that you thought he was out of bounds. But then they put it on the big screen and it was, "Oh my goodness." He always knows exactly where he is on the football field.

That's natural talent. You don't develop that by practicing. The play he made in Philly in 2006 when we played them the second game. Eli pumped the slant to me and Amani ran up the seam and Eli hit him on the money. Amani couldn't have been more than a yard from the back of the end zone. He caught it and didn't even fall down. I was like, "Oh shit, did you see how sweet that was?" Then in 2007 in Atlanta, he had one on the sideline on Monday night on DeAngelo Hall. He ran a come-back-and-go and ran another two yards and broke down. Eli rolled out again, threw it to him, but the ball was out of bounds. Amani stuck his hands out and caught it, foot dragging until the black dirt in the FieldTurf came out.

Now Amani made the one in the Green Bay game on Charles Woodson on the sideline. Another classic for Toom. Those are what we call Teach Tapes. When we're talking about how to do something, we bring out a video of plays like that as a Teach Tape. Green Bay coach Mike McCarthy threw a challenge flag on the play and I was like, "Hey, I don't know why you are throwing a flag, that's Amani Toomer, he does that shit all the time. You better pick it up and put it in your pocket." It's so sweet how he does that that you have no idea how hard it is. That ball he caught on Charles Woodson, Charles had no idea where the ball was. Charles let up because he's like, "Oh, that ball's out of bounds, he's not going to catch that." For me to watch it in person as a receiver, I know how hard it is to do. I give Toom a lot of respect.

So we got the ball to the twelve. Eli hit Amani for another eight yards and then Ahmad Bradshaw got the last four yards and we were up 20–17 late in the third quarter. We got the lead and we were one quarter from making it to the Super Bowl. Green Bay tied it with a field goal early in the fourth and now it was getting pretty intense. It got tougher because on two of the next three drives, our kicker, Lawrence Tynes, missed two field goals, including one to end regulation. We got to a point where they couldn't stop our running game. That's where they really got in trouble. Pound them, pound them, pound them, all the way to the touchdowns. We had them right where we wanted them. We had them in the grinder, man. I call it the grinder when you have a team going like that, and you're running the ball at them, and they can't cover you on the outside. When they can't stop you with an eight-man front, they are in trouble. It's a long day for you.

Our rookie receiver, Steve Smith, was making big catches now. The line was controlling the game. The defense was shutting down Brett Favre. We gotta make these field goals and go home, get our ass to the Super Bowl.

So we were in overtime. Second play for Green Bay, Favre threw an interception to Corey Webster and we were jacked. We got down to their twenty-nine, got stopped, and this time Tynes made the forty-seven-yarder. It was the longest of his three attempts, but he made it and we were outta there and on the way to Phoenix to play New England again. That was a sweet, sweet win just to get to the Super Bowl. But I think beating Dallas in Dallas was probably a bigger win. Dallas was the toughest game we played in the playoffs. It was the third time playing them. We knew the intensity of the game was going to be high and we knew whoever won that game, that team was going to have a shot to get to the Super Bowl. It was easier to get ready for the Green Bay game. We knew it was going to be cold, but we also knew how they were going to play us with their defense. When that game was done, nobody said shit to anybody. We just stormed the field and then ran our asses off the field to get out of the cold.

And get ready for the 18–0 New England Patriots.

17

The Super Bowl

You already know about the roughest part of my Super Bowl week, falling in the shower and hurting my knee. Aside from that, the whole week was crazy, insane. It was the most fun and frustrating week of my life. Dealing with people and tickets—after a while, it was like, just leave me alone, man, I'm trying to sleep, trying to rest. People were crank-calling my room all the time in the middle of the night. I got so many people sending me messages and trying to get ahold of me, it was ridiculous. I had thirty people, friends and family, who came in for the game. They were at a different hotel. Tiffany was at my hotel with Elijah. And the phone wouldn't stop. No lie, I was getting a text message every two minutes, all day long. I had to turn the ringer off. I looked at the phone and thought, *Come on, you can't be for real.*

I was getting so fed up with that, I was ready to go and play the game and go home. It was so bad that when it was Wednesday or Thursday at 9 or 9:30 P.M., I was already in bed. I was exhausted dealing with all that stuff. The only night I went out was Tuesday and I was in by like 1 A.M. or something. After that, I was just concentrating on getting as much rest as I could. I didn't attend one single function other than the media stuff.

Everybody was asking for tickets. I had everybody in my family, high school teammates, my homeboys, everybody was calling. There was one funny one. It was Saturday night and the guys who weren't playing, like the guys on the practice squad, they went out. It was the night before the game and running back Kay-Jay Harris looked at me and said, "You going out with us to this P. Diddy party?" I'm like, "Man, are you crazy? Is something wrong with you? I got the Super Bowl tomorrow." They were cool, they just weren't stressing out. All of them just made the trip to Phoenix and they were having a ball.

The other crazy thing was that people would go downstairs to the front desk and say that they were my relatives and make reservations all over Arizona. They would say, "We're coming to be with Plaxico." These restaurants took reservations under my name from people I don't even know. I found out because I would go downstairs and make dinner reservations every night. It would be like, "I would like to make reservations to go to the City Hall Steakhouse." The concierge would say, "Mr. Burress, you're already having dinner over at Fleming's." I'd say, "What? What you mean?" "Well, somebody came out here and said they are your family member and made reservations for ten people at eight o'clock." I'm like, "No, that wasn't me." Somebody came in and said they were one of my relatives.

And the whole week, all anybody wanted to talk about was the prediction I supposedly made. I was like, yeah, I said it. I'm thinking, *What do you expect me to say?*

But then everybody in the media was saying, "Oh, there go the New York Giants, talking shit again." What did people expect, that we were just going to lay down? We understand the Pats were 18–0 and everything, but they are going to get off their butts and walk into the locker room and put their shoes on just like everyone else. They haven't beaten us yet, and based on the way we played them the first time, it was a three-point game. We got a shot.

Of course the game was pretty slow to start with. People were expecting a lot of scoring, but the defenses were going at it, especially the first half. I caught a fourteen-yard pass on the third play of the game, but that's all I did until the end. That catch got us out of third-and-five and then we keep working it down the field until we get a field goal. We were running the ball pretty good, which you can do on the Patriots if you're patient. We were up 3–0, but New England came back on their first drive, pounding away. They didn't get anything real big, but they got the touchdown.

Pretty much nothing happened in the second quarter. New England got an interception early in the quarter, the first one Eli has thrown in the playoffs. At the end of the quarter, we sacked Tom Brady and forced him into a fumble, which kept them from maybe getting a field goal. It was still 7–3 at halftime and we were doing the usual adjustments. The thing we talked about was sticking with our game plan. We had one turnover, but it didn't hurt us, so we just had to stay patient. But as we were in there, Strahan started talking. He was saying out loud, "We're thirty minutes from a world championship." I think that hit everybody a little. I was there, I just came to a standstill and it hit me, there's just thirty minutes left in the season. I think that put everybody in a state of mind to give it everything we had. Then it got interesting a little at the beginning of the third quarter. The Patriots drove down to our thirty-one and had a fourth-and-thirteen and they went for it instead of kicking the field goal. I was just thinking, hmmm. It's a low-scoring game and all. The rest of the quarter was pretty much the same as the second, trading punts, some sacks, no scoring. But then the fourth quarter started and it became probably the best fourth quarter in the history of the Super Bowl.

Boss made that forty-five-yard catch on our first play of the fourth quarter and all of a sudden it was like, "Hey, we can move the ball fine." Like I said, Boss is nice. Big boy, good hands, and he can run. But he never says nothing, just does his job. That's big for a rookie, especially when you're replacing somebody like Jeremy Shockey. We needed him to come in and handle it. He did. After he made that catch, oh, man, I was personally going over there to pick him up off the ground and shake his hand. I said, "Good job, Boss." He didn't say nothing, that's just how he is. No emotion, just gets the job done.

We got the ball in New England territory, their thirty-five-yard line now, and we kept rolling. We ran Ahmad Bradshaw three times and Eli hit Steve Smith for a big seventeen-yard catch on third-and-four. All of a sudden we got second down at the five-yard line. We ran double slants from the right-hand side with David Tyree in the slot. He got wide open for the touchdown on Asante Samuel. The Patriots just lost him. That was the start of a big day for Tyree. Man, he made history with that catch later on.

Before I get into that, which was crazy, I gotta talk about Tyree. He's a very special person. I don't think I've met a more spiritual guy than Tyree in all of my life. You talk about people talking about it, he lives it 24/7, he walks it. Just being around a person like that, you can't do nothing but just have so much admiration for him and respect for him. The way that he lives his life and the things that he went through before he got to that point. Like I said before, he lost his mom earlier in the year, the night before the Washington game. I cried and hugged him, but I didn't say nothing because I knew there was nothing I could say.

I called him about three days later, gave him time to get

himself together. He came to the phone in great spirits. He was like, "What's up, man? What's going on?" I was just like, damn, "Tyree, what's going on, man? Everything going all right?" He said, "Yeah, man, I'm down in Florida and getting everything together. The funeral is going to be Thursday up in Jersey. I'll see you guys back on Monday." That was the week we played Buffalo, so he missed the Washington game and the Buffalo game, then he was coming right back for the New England game at the end of the season. When he came back Monday and saw us after the Buffalo game, when we were there freezing and grinding it out, he said, "I appreciate how hard you all were working out there, I wish I could have been out there with you all." To see what he went through in that short period of time and the plays that he made, the attitude he had . . . I have so much admiration for him.

Tyree accepts his role, man. He never complains. He's the guy who lifts our wide receiver room. He's always in a good mood. Sometimes Coach Sullivan comes in and he's a little tired, he says, "D.T., go on and give us one, man, we need it. I'm a little tired today, I need it." So David gives us a prayer right there in the meeting. David prays for all of us all the time. Right there in the meeting, he'll just come off the head with one. It's never anything too long, maybe a minute, but just praying for God to individually help each guy have a sharp mind, a great focus on the task at hand. Never anything too heavy or deep. Just what we need to help us get through it. David never complains and he is so family-oriented. You can't ask for a better guy on your team.

What was so crazy about the Super Bowl game was he practiced the Friday before the game and he dropped four or five balls in a row. He couldn't catch a cold in Alaska with two icicles in his hands and a glass of water. The last ball that he caught, guys started clapping like, "Yeah." I said, "Y'all need to cut it out." Antonio Pierce was giving him one of these fake cheers. I said, "Y'all know that's wrong." But to have a practice like that, your last practice of the year, before the biggest game of your life, and you drop four or five balls? That plays with your confidence, it has to a little bit. Practice is what gets you through. Eli just kept telling David, "I'm coming to you, be ready." Then he went in and caught a touchdown, it's just so fitting for him. He is so very deserving of everything that has happened to him, and I'm just so happy for him.

He caught the first touchdown and I was like, "Hey, man, I don't care if I catch a ball. If you can go out and catch some balls and touchdowns and have some successes and we can win, shit, I'm going to act like I had two hundred yards." I was so happy for him. But the best was yet to come.

We got that touchdown with about eleven minutes to go and we were up 10–7. Our defense has just been kicking ass, pounding Brady all game, not letting them run. But those dudes are good over there, so we know we gotta be able to score at some point. Finally, with about eight minutes left, New England got the ball back and drove eighty yards. No big plays, nothing too dramatic, just dinking and dunking down the field until Tom Brady hit Randy Moss for a six-yard touchdown and they were up 14–10. Now we had to get a touchown. No other choice.

We got on the field with 2:39 remaining. We came to the line and I remember I looked over and saw David Diehl, our left tackle, and Richard Seymour of the Patriots talking at each other. They're chopping it up real bad. I'm just sitting there watching them and laughing on a TV time-out. They were just going at it. Then I heard Seymour say, "Hey, I'm going to buy you all some champagne for y'all's ride back home," like we were going to need it after we lose. David said, "Okay, we'll see, we'll see." Seymour and some of those other guys, they were inviting us to their parties. This is with 2:39 left in the game!

We had heard that they had two hundred bottles of champagne on ice already. We heard New England already had parties and stuff lined up for the night. They had it all going on, champagne, parties, they were serious.

We had the ball at our seventeen-yard line, so we were backed up pretty good. Everybody was confident when Eli hits Amani for eleven yards. But then Eli tried to throw to me on first and second down and both were incomplete. Now we had third-and-ten at the two-minute warning. We were pretty much in a two-down situation. The other thing was that Diehl looked like he was getting tired, so we were getting him help on the pass rush over on that side. Somehow, we had to get New England back on their heels because this was where they could do a bunch of blitzing and shit they like to do.

So Eli hit Amani for nine yards to get us to fourth-and-one. Jacobs powered up on the fourth down to get two yards and now we were at our own thirty-nine with 1:28 left. We had a lot of time to start the drive, but now it was starting to get dicey with the clock. We still had all our time-outs, so it wasn't desperate, but we had to start getting in position. On first down, Eli scrambled for five yards when the pass play wasn't there right away. The first time-out got used to stop the clock. Next, Eli went deep down the right side for Tyree for an incomplete and now we were in third-and-five with 1:15 left. It was still a two-down situation, just like on third-and-ten a few plays before.

Now comes the play for history. I talked about Tyree a little before, but I didn't talk about his hands. He has some strong hands. We call him "Lay Hands Inc." because when he gets those hands on you, he ain't letting go. We put him in a lot for blocking on our run plays. He gets in there on linebackers, he gets in there on the big boys, linebackers and strong safeties like Roy Williams. He gets up on those boys and *boom*, if he gets his hands inside of you, it's like vise grips. You're not getting off. He'll turn you and throw you down on the ground. This time, he got his hands on that football and wouldn't let it go.

I was on the left side, and I released outside to help clear out the middle. Tyree was on the right and ran in. I see Tyree and then I looked at Eli and I thought Eli was sacked. There was just a bunch of jerseys surrounding him. But both of the defensive linemen got on his shoulder and he rolled out. Then I saw him get ready to fire it downfield and I was like, "No." I looked over at David Tyree and I saw Rodney Harrison coming from behind and Eli threw it. I just sat there and watched it and I watched David Tyree plant his feet and just go up and grab the ball with two hands. I never saw the helmet part because I was on the other side. But what I did see was him fighting for the ball. When he hit the ground, the ball couldn't have been no farther than two inches from the ground, but it never touched the ground.

I was like, "Holy shit, he caught it!" The next thing in the huddle, I grabbed him by his head and I said, "Man, you just saved the fucking Super Bowl." He laughed and said, "I don't know what's going on." His eyes were just looking around, wondering. I've been in a lot of football games, and I've *never* heard a crowd light up like that. A lot of people say they don't hear the crowd when they are playing, but it was so loud that it was like even the New England fans couldn't believe it. If you don't have any appreciation for that play, for him making that play, you're just not a fan of football. It was so tense that I couldn't even laugh, but that's exactly what came out of his mouth, "I don't know what's going on." David Tyree, with everything that had happened to that young man over the past few months, there was nobody more deserving of the things that's happened to him, the recognition, everything that he is getting from the outside. It's very well deserved.

Now we were at the New England twenty-four-yard line

and I was thinking, *We're going to win this game.* We used our second time-out to stop the clock and then Eli got sacked trying to scramble away. It was only a one-yard loss, but still we used our last time-out. The next pass went toward Tyree, but it was incomplete. Now it was third-and-eleven. Eli hit Steve Smith on the right side as he was rolling that way. Sweet throw, sweet catch, and Smith got out of bounds to stop the clock with thirty-nine seconds left.

That's where I came in against Hobbs. I was thinking they'd put two defenders on the back side to handle me. There's no way they don't. We had three receivers on the other side. But they were setting up to blitz and I saw the coverage. I was like, *Holy shit, they're going to do this.* From earlier in the week, I had studied Hobbs and knew if I gave him a hard fake on the slant, he would go for it. All of a sudden it's "Hike," and there I go to catch the game-winning touchdown. I haven't done anything all game, but here I am. I just remember after the game was over, I looked over and Junior Seau was out there, laying on the ground with his head buried in the turf so deep you couldn't even see his face. He was way down. I don't think those guys could believe that we could drive the field like that against them at the end of the game. They were just stunned. As we were leaving the field, I don't even remember shaking hands with any of the Patriots. We got no love after that one. That's happened in some other games, like when I was in Pittsburgh and we played Baltimore. There was no love in that one, either.

It was unbelievable. We were up 17–14. Our defense got on the field for the last four plays. They sacked Brady on second down and then he threw two incompletes to Moss. Both of those looked close at the end, but we had two guys on Moss. We ran the last play with one second left and we were champions. I can't explain that feeling, man. I went over and found my family. I held Elijah above my head. I was crying. It was amazing.

From there, it was just crazy. We were screaming and hollering, having a great time. We all got back to the locker room and it was packed with people. We were trying to get showers, do interviews, get dressed, see family. It was like I couldn't see straight. It was wonderful, total chaos. Finally, I saw one of our owners, John Mara. I smiled. He came up to me and said, "Great game." He was real quiet about it and then he said, "Next year, no predictions." He just kind of laughed and walked off, but I could tell he was serious about that.

That's fine, no more predictions.

18

Chillin' with Bill

So it was a few weeks after we won the Super Bowl and I was back in South Florida. Someone called my financial adviser, Jeff Rubin, and they invited me to this political fund-raiser in Boca Raton where former president Bill Clinton was speaking. So I had lunch with Bill Clinton. It was crazy. He's a cool dude, man. I walked up to him, it's a nice house, pool, everything. He was giving a little speech. I came in and he talked me up and it's almost like I was the show. It seemed like people were happier to see me than Bill. It got so crazy, I was taking so many pictures. Then I was dealing with the Secret Service. You had to have a name tag on and if you said you wanted to go somewhere, you had to be cleared by the government. They had Secret Service everywhere. Everywhere. So I went over there, signed some autographs and took pictures, and then they put me in this little room, like this gazebo, where Bill was going to be at after the speech. So I saw him. He said to some other people, "Hey, I want you to meet my good friend, the world champion Plaxico Burress." I haven't even introduced myself to him yet, but he just sees me and introduces me.

So we were sitting there talking and he shook my hand for

like ten minutes. We're just talking. I'm thinking, *Yeah, okay, Bill, you can let go of my hand now*. He was saying, "It was so inspiring what you guys did for us in New York, all the things that we've been through, 9/11. You guys just personified the real New York City attitude. You just make so many people proud to be New Yorkers. We really needed that. You guys inspired a lot of people in that city. I was just so happy to call myself a New Yorker." He's shaking my hand the whole time. I'm still thinking, *All right, man, you can let go of my hand now*. It was cool, I got to meet Bill and have a couple of glasses of wine. It was top shelf. He gave me his card and said, "If you ever want to come to D.C. and check out the Secret Service facility and where their training facility is, give me a call and I'll make sure you get clearance right on through." I'm like, "All right, Bill, pleasure to meet you, dog." I heard Bill is cool like that. I was like, "I'll do that number, I'm going to holler at you, man. All right, man. Peace." Bill Clinton, cool as a fan. I'd love to sit down with a bottle with him and hang out. I got to chop it up with Bill Clinton, that's the best thing to happen so far.

I'm not political at all, but as we're there, one of the senators who was there said, "Now you can change your vote." He just assumed I was voting for Obama. We didn't even talk about it. I thought, *Damn, whoever it was automatically thinks that's how I'm voting*. I looked at Jeff when we were coming back and said, "Wow, that's crazy." I didn't think people on that level assumed like that. He just put me in there. I should have said some crazy shit like, "No, I'm voting for McCain." But that just threw me for a loop. Me and Jeff talked about it all the way out. I was like, "Man, can you believe him saying that shit?" That's sad. Really sad.

Now, I'm going to vote for Obama, but I don't believe that he'll really get elected. What I say is, I'll believe it when he gets elected. I don't believe it's going to happen. I'm just telling you.

I gotta see it for my own self to believe it. It ain't easy to get all those delegate votes. I gotta see it for myself. If he gets elected, man, could be some crazy shit happenin' at the White House. Jay-Z knockin' on the White House door. Diddy walkin' through the White House. Oprah is going to have her own fucking room in there. Everybody should be able to get into the White House. "Hey, Obama, Plax out here." I'm just telling you what's going to happen. Everybody is going to think it's cool just to walk up to the White House. Man, that shit ain't cool, you'll get your ass blasted. I would love to be Secret Service, because their clearance is green light. They're some bad boys. They're looking for someone to jump on. That'll be some funny shit.

Okay, that's the fun part. But there was a lot of work. Most days, I was standing in the middle of Joe Caroccio's clinic in Davie, Florida, and I hate this shit. He was making me do all sorts of lifts and stretches and exercises that hurt like hell. I did this for about two hours a day three days a week. Had to do it, but I hate it. Not so much because it hurts. My ankle and my knee are weak, so I have to get myself ready. No choice. And the knee is getting better. They tell me the ankle will scar up, so no surgery on that. No surgery on anything—knee, ankle, or shoulder. I don't need to do my pinkie, either. Looks weird, but it doesn't affect my ability to catch.

Right after we got back from the Super Bowl, we were all supposed to go to the parade in New York, but the doctors told me to stay away. That's how banged up I was. They didn't want it to get any worse. I couldn't run for three months because of the ankle and I just needed to rest anyway. Some guys get right back from the season and want to start working out two weeks later. When I'm done with football, I like to get away, but it was hard to do this year because of the Super Bowl. When the season was done, I wanted to get so far away it was not even funny. I didn't want to walk in the weight room or nothing. I just wanted to get away and rejuvenate and relax. Then, when it would be time for me to go, I'd be fresh and ready. I can't be around football and all that. It will wear you out, man, 'cause it's on your mind constantly. That is one of the reasons I've never lived in the off-season in the city I played in. I don't even have pictures of me playing football in my house down in Florida. Nothing except the picture of me when I was twelve years old with my uniform on, back when it got started.

Still, I had to do the physical therapy and it was getting better. But it hurt. After only like five minutes, I was breaking out in a sweat. In the off-season before 2007, I couldn't even get up on my toes for six or seven months because of my ankle surgery. This year, I'm starting to heal up and getting my strength back. The physical therapy is the first step. The worst is this toe raise I do where I put pressure on different parts of my foot. It helps protect against sprains and that was pretty big for me last year. Joe always wants me to do the things I'm not good at so I can get stronger.

I don't want to be bad at anything, but those drills that I do over there, they're the worst. I look like I'm just not an athletic guy, and I don't like looking like that. But it helps me so much, breaking and coming out of my route. Last year Joey worked me so hard. He took my ankle, the one I had surgery on, and then the same thing I had to do with my left ankle, I had to do with my right ankle. I said, "Joey, why am I doing these things with my right ankle? It's my left one that's hurting." He said, "You need to work on both of them the same." I said, "No, I don't, it's my left ankle that's hurting." Sure as shit, I hurt the other one this year. Joey was right. Once I'm healthy and I get strong again, I can't wait to get back to playing games. I've been working at this for a few years now and I know the benefits of what I'm doing.

The good thing for me is I don't really get out of shape. I maybe put on four or five pounds at the most. Everybody will say, "You're not working out yet?" When I start working out, I work so hard I can get myself into shape in two weeks. So I don't need to run right now. I do so much running during the season. As I'm writing this, in the middle of March, I need to relax. The season has been over for like five weeks. Some guys, like San Francisco running back Frank Gore, have been working out for like six, seven weeks already. Frank is busting his ass all over. I say, "What are you doing, man?" He's like, "I'm trying to get it, I want to get back." In the first week of March? Then he told me he's been working out since two weeks after the season ended. You gotta rest your body. We all want to have a great season. Everybody is going after the same thing. But I believe in rest.

When I get back, it's running for me. I'm going to get back in shape in two and a half or three weeks and I'm ready to go. It's not like I'm going to be getting thirty pounds overweight like some of the linemen. When I work out, man, I consider myself one of the hardest workers. When the other guys are going down in their workout, I'll be coming back, laughing at them. Once I start working out, I don't know how to stop. I'm there three or four hours. When I come home, I tell Tiffany, "If I don't come home and take a nap, then I didn't work hard enough." When I come home, I go throw a sweaty bag of clothes on her and she goes, "Eww." Damn, I sweat. You can squeeze them and they run like water out of them. I tell her, "Yeah, that's what I'm out there doing while you're walking around over there in the Boca Mall in the Gucci store looking for some jeans." She looks at me and says, "That's nasty." I said, "Yeah, this is what I'm doing. I'm working."

I've heard people say that receivers are prima donnas and artists. I tell you what, catching a ball is an art. I always said, for whatever you try to do the best, you have to do the most you can to get better. I respect my craft. Playing wide receiver is a craft, it's an art. I know I will never be able to be perfect, but I know the closer I get to perfect, I'm getting better. The thing is you can't be scared if you're going to play that position. You can't show fear. You have to have a different type of attitude when you approach the game. Any receiver that says they don't want to get over a hundred yards and a touchdown every Sunday, they're lying. When you play receiver, you want to have a big game every week, be on that stage and show yourself.

When you're an athlete and people see you around, they can't believe it's you. It's like, "You're not Plaxico Burress, are you? Oh man!" People just get moved when they meet you or when they see you. I try to just be as normal as I possibly can, but people put you way up here on a pedestal like you are not even human. You can see how much of an impact we have on people. It's incredible for something that I do, and people watch. Some people really genuinely love you as a football player. It's probably not fair, but you see how much people are moved and how much influence you have on people's lives just by playing football. I never really was able to understand that. Some people are actually crazy.

I guess you could say that in some way, I live some people's dreams. I dreamed of playing in the NFL, too. But I can't see myself walking up to people and just being in disbelief. It's crazy. People from my old neighborhood don't even act like that. You think that they would be the worst, but they are like, "He's one of the first people that made it out." They actually are the ones who treat me closest to normal as far as anybody when I'm home. You meet people just going out, whew, man. In stores, restaurants, getting gas. People won't let you be normal. You can't live a normal life. We got cars, nice cribs, and all of that, but the people on the outside won't let you be normal. They put you on the shelf, box you up, and put you in the house. I'm not comfortable with it, fame and how to deal with all of that. What we do just has so much effect on that.

This is what I really hate. Someone will recognize you and they'll be like, "Hey, Plaxico, can I get an autograph for my daughter." Yeah, sure, no problem. But then somebody else will come up to you right after that and say, "I'm sorry I don't know who you are, but you look famous. Can I get your autograph?" How do people get the audacity to say things like that. "I don't know who you are, but you look famous." Damn.

Other people come up and tell me all the time, "I never thought you would have been this way." I say, "What you mean?" "Oh, you look so intimidating." They tell me I don't smile, that I'm unapproachable. I don't take anything from it, that's just how I have been perceived. It doesn't have anything to do with the kind of person that I am. I don't waste a lot of time trying to explain who I am to them or to the media. That stuff just gets too frustrating. The media writes one thing about me and all of a sudden that's all that anybody knows. I can get frustrated trying to explain myself. I've seen it happen to so many guys. That's why you see so many guys who are so inconsistent from week to week. They get caught up in what the media is saying and they lose focus.

What it is for all of us as players, as it is for anyone really, you want to be recognized for what you do. Everybody in this world wants to be recognized for what they do. We all want to be successes, that is our motivation. We strive to be great and make as much money as we can. When you are recognized for what you do, all that stuff comes. It doesn't matter if you're a player or anything else. If you're a drug dealer, you want to be known as the guy who has the best marijuana. Landscapers, the guy who is my power washer, people in sales, people who can drink the most Hennessey. I see it all the time. Everybody wants to be known for something.

For me, I don't try to fight the battle with the media. People aren't in the locker room to get to know me as a person, so why try to fight that battle? I just focus on trying to be the best receiver. That's my job, to play my ass off.

ACKNOWLEDGMENTS

At the end of one of the early interviews, Plaxico said something to the effect that you learn a lot more by listening than by talking. That seems to embody much of what he is about, much of that coming from his mother's grace, power, and pride. So first and foremost, I'm grateful to Plaxico for allowing me to listen and learn while he talked.

There are many others who helped with this project, starting with Robert Bailey from Rosenhaus Sports, and Ian Kleinert and Jarred Weisfeld from Objective Entertainment, believing it could be done so quickly. A special thanks to Mike Garafolo, the sharp and energetic Giants beat writer for the *Newark Star-Ledger*, who should have been the one to write this book but wasn't allowed to because of company policy. Mike was exceptionally generous with ideas and information about Burress, with whom he has developed a stunning professional relationship. Further thanks to the other Giants beat writers, such as Ralph Vacchiano, John Branch, Paul Schwartz, and Vinny Di-Trani, whose work I leaned on. Giants general manager Jerry Reese was generous with his time, as was Giants vice president of communications Pat Hanlon. There were plenty of people who did the hard time on this project, starting with the quick transcribing of Julie Cole and Jill May. Editor Doug Grad of HarperCollins was extraordinary throughout. Finally, thanks to Alana McNamara for her patience and to Elijah for allowing me to borrow his dad for many hours.